Enrollment and the Christian School:
EXTENDING GOD'S KINGDOM

Enrollment and the Christian School:
EXTENDING GOD'S KINGDOM

by Simon Jeynes, MEd, MA
Executive Director, Christian School Management

partnership · leadership · transformation

XULON PRESS

Xulon Press
2301 Lucien Way #415
Maitland, FL 32751
407.339.4217
www.xulonpress.com

Christian School Management
20 Kyle Drive, Ridgetown, Ontario, Canada N0P2C0
Text: (519) 401-2351
Web: www.christianschoolmanagement.org
E-mail: christianschoolmanagement@gmail.com

Disclaimer: Christian School Management Association is a Christian nonprofit 501(c)(3) organization providing teaching and training to Christian private-independent school leaders and faculty. CSM is not a law firm. No service or information provided by CSM should be construed as legal advice.

Unless otherwise indicated, Scripture quotations taken from the Holy Bible, New International Version (NIV). Copyright © 1973, 1978, 1984, 2011 by Biblica, Inc.™. Used by permission. All rights reserved.

Printed in the United States of America.

Paperback ISBN-13: 978-1-6322-1376-1
eBook ISBN-13: 978-1-6322-1377-8

Mission

For Jesus, through mission, with students

Vision

A Christian education for children everywhere

Motto

"On earth as it is in heaven" (Matthew 6)

Key Words

Partnership, Leadership, Transformation

Table of Contents

Book Reviews

"Simon Jeynes' book on Christian school enrollment has hit upon a key ingredient of our work in the Christian school...being the 'doorkeeper' of God's Kingdom in the education of young people. This is not just Hallmark sentiment, but involves purpose, process, and a partnership that begins and ends with admissions. The "who," "how," and "why" of enrollment is the initial step in our kingdom mission around the kingdom message of reconciliation of faith and learning. Simon addresses, with his straightforward, reasoned manner, what our Christian schools must weigh in these days, to be relevant promotors of God's purposes here on earth, as it is in heaven."

-Bill Stevens, Executive Director,
Mid-Atlantic Christian School Association

"Covering an integral piece of Christian schools that often is overlooked, *Enrollment and the Christian School* by Simon Jeynes is an excellent book for any Christian school leader looking to ensure there is an intentional, mission driven approach when it comes to enrollment at their school. Too often the enrollment process is a "wait and see" approach, but this book shows a vast array of items that can support a school's enrollment growth. Items ranging from a yearly enrollment calendar, an emphasis on the importance of students, staff, and parents in the enrollment process, and examples of how to organize enrollment data, this book contains a multitude of ready-to-implement enrollment materials and action steps that can be immediately placed within a school. I highly recommend Christian school leaders have this book on their shelf as they seek to fulfill, and grow, their school's mission through enrollment!"

-Tyler Van Schepen, Superintendent and Principal,
Traverse City Christian School

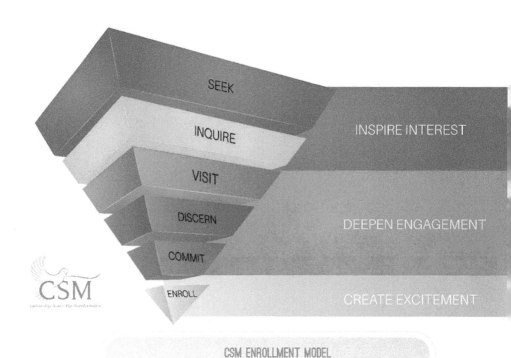

SEEK

INQUIRE — INSPIRE INTEREST

VISIT

DISCERN — DEEPEN ENGAGEMENT

COMMIT

ENROLL — CREATE EXCITEMENT

CSM

CSM ENROLLMENT MODEL

Preface

This book is dedicated to Principals who work so hard and worry so much about their enrollment from January to September. I have worked with Principals / Heads of School across the country who need to know that God is a God of many blessings and that their labor in the field, when mission directed, Scripturally infused, research based, and experientially understood will be 'rewarded' and counted to them as righteousness.

I dedicate this book to the many Admission Directors I have known – although CSM now calls them Family Relationship Managers – who have informed me about their practices, educated me out of many of my errors (though alack, not out of all), and been steadfast in the journey.

I am deeply thankful to Terri Gillespie, editor extraordinaire, who has saved this book from many unfortunate issues thus making it infinitely more readable. I must say too, that she forced me to rethink some ideas and add sections ensuring that the book made some sense. Any errors are entirely my fault.

As always, and with no less a sense of gratitude because of that, I thank my family who frequently note my obsessiveness, wonder why I am writing on a Saturday afternoon when we should be playing together, and put up with my stress whenever I am behind in my work. They have caused me to change my opinions, my attitudes, and my behavior for the better – at least to the extent that they could. I am grateful to Carolynn, Alexis, Brendan, Jared, and Kristen, not to mention our pets who waited for me to take them for walks on many occasions.

I hope this book is a blessing to you, its readers, and to your schools that will be fuller as a result. If not, I have failed. But I am confident enough (my enemies say arrogant enough) to believe that the advice herein will truly be helpful to you as you contend with the darts of the enemy and surround more and more children with the love and joy of being followers of Jesus, to whom be glory for ever and ever, Amen.

All Biblical citations (unless otherwise noted) are from the New International Version.

Introduction

Welcome to CSM's book on enrollment and the Christian school. CSM was founded, in part, on the premise that the Christian School Movement lacked vigor and direction in addressing the disturbing evidence that many of our schools were closing and maybe even more were struggling on an annual basis. From 2003 onward, there was a discernible decline in the number of Christian schools and in the number of children enrolled in Christian schools. Since 2015, there has been a small recovery but not to the extent of reversing the decline, even as the number of children in the United States and Canada continues to grow.

In the research done by Barna, Cardus and others, there remain questions about the effectiveness of Christian education: is it too holy and not academic enough? Is it too academic and not holy enough? What does it mean to attempt to be excellent both in spiritual formation and academic preparation? What exactly are we preparing our children for? Only if we can formulate convincing and persuasive arguments to answer these questions can we hope to look at the long-term health of Christian schools with optimism. In a society that is not as comfortable for Christians as it used to be, the assumption that we will always be here must be questioned.

But CSM approaches the task of enrollment, including both retention and recruitment of students, with enormous hope. We believe in a resurrection God. We have the witness of the first century A.D. and the enormous impact that Jesus had in a hostile environment as the church grew (unexpectedly) over the first four centuries to become the dominant religious force in both west and east empires. We know how attractive the words of Jesus are to a world seeking meaning, relationship, intimacy, purpose, and self-fulfillment.

Our schools must embrace change as Christianity always has, even if sometimes reluctantly. Our schools must reach out to seek all kinds of families, not just the comfortable ones that look and speak and worship like us. Our schools must be models of excellence. Our schools must be the light on the hill in our neighborhoods and regions. If we do that, retention and recruitment of students is assured.

This book can be read from beginning to end or dipped into. We recommend reading all of it first, even though there is some redundancy. We welcome you as a reader and practitioner and pray that this book provides illustration, inspiration, and insight. May God bless you and the school you lead that you may be better equipped as a result of our work.

Retention:
The Foundation of Enrollment

Definition

Retention is the ability of the Christian school to have a powerful enough witness to its children and parents so that those families are persuaded to stay at the school rather than move to a competitive alternative.

- If your retention rate is less than 85%, your school will decline.
- If your retention rate is 90%, your school is in good shape.
- If your retention rate is 95%+, your school is excellent.

Retention rate is calculated using the following formula:

> Total number of students returning from one year to the next divided by total students minus graduating students minus students whose families are moving out of area.

Data

It is rather disconcerting to visit many Christian schools where retention data is not tracked with great attention to detail. Some schools are not paying attention to their admission data either. It is critical to have good data so that you can really force great conversations that question assumptions and lead to powerful strategic actions. CSM routinely goes to schools where the following kind of statements are made:

- Families love our school.
- We have a wonderful community here.
- Everyone is going in the same direction.
- The teachers are godly, excellent people.
- We truly experience God's grace here.

Of course, we would hope that this would be true of all schools. These are important statements to be able to make about one's school. We, also routinely, ask what the evidence for these statements is. This question can be seen as a cross between mildly threatening and downright contentious. Christian schools don't often have robust conversations about things they believe should be taken for granted. All too often, there is very little data to support these statements. We hasten to add that doesn't mean they are untrue. It means that they are unsupported. And therein lies a problem. What if they are not true or, at least, not fully true?

In the context of this book, there is, unfortunately, often a disconnect between these statements and the enrollment trends at the school. Schools that portray themselves as wonderful communities of excellent learning can also be experiencing a decade or more of enrollment decline. Here is an example of one such school:

2012-13	173
2013-14	150
2014-15	163
2015-16	131
2016-17	117
2017-18	111

Here is a six-year decline of 36% that should have caught everyone's attention. The only real attention paid at the school was to the budget bottom-line. And urging the Principal to get more students. It took a lot of work to be able to identify the numbers that needed to be looked at. What were the issues? Why was there a loss of students? What could make that change? What contributed to the issue?

Why is there sometimes almost a resistance to collecting data, to counting, to making lists? Maybe at your school, it's not an issue. If it is, we urge you to keep data assiduously. To be a data hound is not to lack faith. It is to understand that we are whole people and need prayer and 2,000 calories a day to have a healthy life – one is not antithetical to the other.

What data should we collect? How many students you have is certainly a beginning, but only a beginning.

Why Enrollment Numbers Don't Tell the Whole Story

The next level of sophistication is to know which students returned from last year and which are new, that is, to understand your retention data as well as your admission data. It may seem strange to begin with retention in a book on enrollment. Isn't enrollment about the Admission Director and Principal bringing in students to the school? Well, yes, of course. It also makes sense to acknowledge that keeping students who are already in the school is of even higher priority than bringing them in. Let's look at the enrollment numbers for a Christian school and see what they can tell us. This is a K–8 school and shows enrollment from 1980 to 2016.

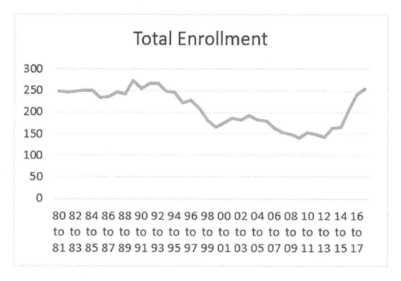

This is an interesting chart for all kinds of reasons:

- Enrollment was relatively stable in the '80s.
- Enrollment dramatically declined in the '90s.
- It recovered slightly in the 2000s and then continued the decline (not connected to the 2008–09 depression!).
- Over the past five years, it has seen a strong recovery.

The chart tells a story, but it is an extremely vague one. We don't know the reasons for the general decline; we don't know the reasons for the specific ups and downs; the chart can't tell us why the school seems suddenly to be doing so much better. The numbers themselves don't tell us much. They provoke a lot of questions but answer almost none except the raw numbers themselves. Retention is a big part of the answer. Let's look at a different school and the way it organized its data:

	Old Year Enrollment	Not returned	Returned	Retention Percentage	New Year Enrollment	Total Enrolled
K	25				24	24
1	28	7	18	72.0%	4	22
2	24	4	24	85.7%	4	28
3	26	3	21	87.5%	3	24
4	21	4	22	84.6%	4	26
5	26	1	20	95.2%	3	23
6	19	3	23	88.5%	6	29
7	21	5	14	73.7%	5	19
8	22	2	19	90.5%	0	19
9	31	3	19	86.4%	7	26
10	27	1	30	96.8%	1	31
11	18	2	25	92.6%	1	26
12		0	18	100.0%	0	18
Total	288	35	253	87.8%	62	315
with 12th	310					

This is a K – 12 school. The first column (Old Year Enrollment) tells us the number of students who were in the class last year. The third column (Returned) tells us how many returned to the next grade, e.g., there were 25 students last year in K and 18 of them returned for first grade. The fourth column creates a percentage return rate. There are an equal number of grades where the retention percentage is in the 80% – 90% range and in the 90% –100% range. There are a couple of grades where it is below 80%. Overall, the retention percentage is 87.8%, which is slightly below the "good shape" metric of 90%.

Note, however, that the actual enrollment goes up from 310 to 315, and this number would suggest to the casual observer that all was well. The school has done an excellent job of recruiting 62 new students. Total enrollment is up and the budget looks really good. Retention statistics give the Finance Committee pause for thought, however. It would be wise not to assume that this financial wind-fall will be repeated in subsequent years. With a retention under 90%, and with two grades under 80%, there are clearly questions that need to be asked and answered.

Note: enrollment data is always compared from year to year at the same time, typically two weeks into the school year; retention data is compared from the end of one school year to the beginning of the next school year – first day of class.

The Four Keys to Retention

It used to be that once you had a student in the school, you would keep that child forever unless something really bad happened. This is a 20th century idea that is not relevant in the 21st century. In today's family, the decision to re-enroll is made on an annual basis at every grade level. A family enrolling a child in Kindergarten will make an enrollment decision 12 times before that child heads off on the next stage of the journey. How does a family make that decision? There are four keys to retention:

1. The first key to retention is the child. Later in admission, we will share survey data showing that students have powerful decision-making capacity over which school to attend. There is now significant survey data showing that right down to Kindergarten, the child is being given a voice. Certainly as the child grows older, that voice can act both as a veto as well as an encouragement for. Simply put, if the child does not want to go to your school, the child will be invited to voice that opinion and, if strongly enough held, that opinion will be decisive. On the other hand, if the parent wants to take the child out of the school,

the child also has a veto vote on staying – there have been numerous one-to-one conversations with parents where they admitted to not being that happy with the school but the daughter or son refuses to leave. The child is influenced by three things:

- a relationship with a key adult
- a positive peer group (or sub-group of students) that is going in the same direction, more or less
- an alignment of the school with at least one major interest of the child

Where none of these are true, the child will leave. Where one or two are true, the school has a better than average chance of keeping the child. Where all three are true, the child is an advocate for the school.

2. The second key is the teacher. The relationship between a teacher and a student is the biggest in-school predictor of both academic success and emotional / spiritual satisfaction. This question should be asked four weeks into the year: who is advocating for each child in the school. Who has a relationship with that child? Who is being missed? The child being missed is more often than not your retention issue. While we cannot mandate relationship, the school must hire and retain teachers who have an attitude that impels them to go out and meet the child, not stand still and expect the child to come to them. This is so in both academic and emotional / spiritual areas. Academically, it is seen when a teacher accepts the child's academic position and then works individually to bring that child to where he or she needs to be. Emotionally / spiritually, it is seen when the teacher approaches the child to ask how they are, or is open and willingly gives time when approached by the child.

3. The third key is the school's mission. If the mission is known by all members of the school community and embedded into daily life, the child will experience certainty, collective purpose, and personal meaning. A mission that is alive in the corridors, classrooms, playing fields, performance halls, awards ceremonies has a strong attraction for the child. On the other hand, a mission not clearly articulated, variably lived out by the adults in the school, not used as a beacon to follow or inform, is a mission that has no collective efficacy and leaves the child at the whim of each situation.

4. The final key is the school's relationship with the family. This is developed more fully in the next section – simply, the parents must also be engaged. The school must not assume that parents know anything more than the school has told them. Parents also want to be "visible."

Retention is an ongoing process. You must never take either the child or the parent or the family as a whole for granted. The moment they become invisible is the moment of your gravest danger. In this sense, the loud parent is very helpful since that parent is making you aware of issues that other parents are likely to be concerned about. The invisible parent vanishes before you even knew there was a concern. The program for retention is as intentional as the program for admission.

So What Is Our Relationship to Parents in Our Christian Schools?

This is of necessity a complex topic with so many variants across cultures, theologies, geographies, and school missions that it almost seems foolish to attempt. But attempt we must because both our families and our schools who serve them have lost our way in that relationship. Let's start with a conventional Christian school mission (a real one) that can be replicated across hundreds if not thousands of our schools:

> CSM Christian School supports families in equipping children to reach God's standard of spiritual maturity and academic excellence, training them to influence their world from a biblical perspective.

Whether the mission statement declares it or not, Christian schools universally recognize that the parents have the right and responsibility to raise up their children. As Psalm 127 says: Children are a heritage from the Lord. And Colossians 3 at least outlines the relationship between parents and children – obedience from children and encouragement from parents. This is paralleled in the United Nations Convention on the Rights of the Child from 1989 in Article Five:

> States Parties shall respect the responsibilities, rights and duties of parents or, where applicable, the members of the extended family or community as provided for by local custom, legal guardians or other persons legally responsible for the child, to provide, in a manner consistent with the evolving capacities of the child, appropriate direction and guidance in the exercise by the child of the rights recognized in the present Convention.[1]

It is well established in biblical example and teaching, as well as in international law, that the parent has the prior right and responsibility to educate the child. But when the parents contract with the Christian school for the school to educate the child – recognizing that this contract is to some extent involuntary since the state requires that the child attend a school (see note at end) – then in what sense is the school partnering with rather than taking over important aspects of the child's upbringing?

We should acknowledge that it is not partnering in any usual sense of the term. There is no doubt that the parents send their children to the school entirely on the school's terms. The parents acknowledge this in the contract they sign, in the statement of faith they affirm, in the practices of their own household, in the calendar they follow, and in the daily routines of the family. All is on the school's terms. If it is a partnership, there is very definitely a senior and a junior partner.

In the 20th century, this reality was almost entirely hidden because, in most Christian schools, the purpose of the school was to be the third rail of the church / family/ school triangle. The family went to the church that sponsored the school. This is true across all denominations, whether Catholic, evangelical, Lutheran, Episcopal / Anglican, etc. There was an unspoken alignment that was intentional and prized. Indeed, not always to our credit, our schools also often served as insulation from societal movements that we did not support in the lives of our children. This included racial, social, economic, religious fault lines that divided us increasingly from each other. *Our Kids* by Robert Putnam (2015)[2] shows that those fault lines seemed less apparent 50 years ago, and that today they have become emblematic of American society (and have echoes in Canadian society as well). He writes in his introduction (edited): "In the 1950s most families consisted of a breadwinner dad, a homemaker mom, and the kids, a stable union. This collapsed in the 1970s and the result was a novel two-tier pattern of family structure that is still with us today" (pp. 61/63). The two tiers were a neo-traditional college-educated tier, although with both parents working, and the fragile tier of families with no more than high school education. The latter are today characterized by economic hardship, single parenting, higher divorce rates, cohabitation, children born outside marriage.

In the 21st century, those fault lines and the breakdown in the church / family / school paradigm have become increasingly apparent even though most of our parents are in the neo-traditional family model, and this is what leads to the question about our relationship with our children. Here are some examples of the breakdown:

- In 1950, 20% of marriages ended in divorce; today, it's approximately 40%.
- Four in 10 American children are now born to unmarried mothers, up from about 5% in 1960.
- Christian church membership is declining as the Pew Research diagram on the left shows.

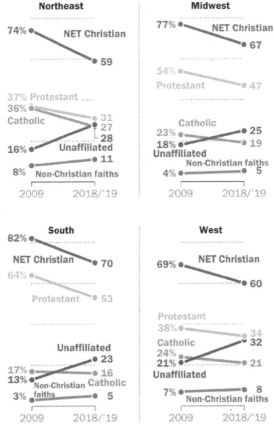

Catholic share down 9 points in Northeast; Protestants down 11 in South

% of U.S. adults who identify as ...

Source: Aggregated Pew Research Center political surveys conducted 2009 and January 2018-July 2019 on the telephone. "In U.S., Decline of Christianity Continues at Rapid Pace"

PEW RESEARCH CENTER

- In 1970, 84% of U.S. children spent their entire childhoods living with both bio-parents. Today, only half can expect to do the same.
- The percentage of childless women doubled between the 1970s and 2005.
- Loneliness is on the upswing: "Loneliness among older adults is a growing population health threat...recent declines in marriage, increases in gray divorce, and fertility decline are leading to larger numbers of older adults with no close family members."[3]
- Christian churches are largely unwilling, unless they are the school's owners, to publicly support the Christian school "against" the public school.
- Christian churches are no longer providing all, or even most, of the students for the Christian school.
- Christian churches are generally aging with fewer families.
- Christian churches are not providing the financial resources they used to; it is no longer unusual in church schools for the church to begin looking at the school as a source of revenue.
- More and more church schools are becoming independent organizations with a self-sustaining Board.
- Christian schools that rely exclusively on their churches for students, or that rely on a single confessional client base are going out of business – there is just not a large enough demographic.
- Christian schools are pulling from a far wider field and, increasingly, from the non-Christian marketplace that is attracted to the Christian sense of values and consistency.
- The "Fragile Families and Wellbeing Study" finds that children in unstable families are the ones that do worst.[4]
- At the same time, there is a growing body of research led and inspired by Suniya Luthar showing how adolescents from high-income households have higher levels of substance abuse than low-income families. These children show a disturbing lack of intimacy within their families as well as a heightened sense of peer envy in a highly

competitive school environment directly influenced by a school stress on summative forms of evaluation.

What can schools do? More importantly, what is it that we now HAVE to do in order to meet the needs of our families? The Barna 2019 research "Households of Faith"[5] talks about the Vibrant Household and notes (p. 122) that it cuts across kinds of families – nuclear, single-parent, multi-generational, roommate, couple, and other. The characteristics of the vibrant family include the following (pp. 124-5):

- spends fun, quality time together
- welcomes others
- asks for help
- members have a personal spirituality
- a spiritual coach is present

We can also identify healthy and powerful attitudes that schools can share with parents that will have a positive influence on their children. In a 2016 study ("A New Framework for Understanding Parent Involvement")[6], students in focus groups identified four themes of "successful" parenting:

1. Their parents were *supportive,* not just in their schooling but in their extracurricular activities. Their parents did not micromanage their academic lives.
2. Parents *skillfully navigated school choices.*
3. Parents *effectively conveyed the importance of school,* often in a manner that might lead their children to make academic success central to their purpose in life. Their parents also provided clear examples of the undesirable outcomes of not taking school seriously.
4. Parents gave them the *label of being smart* that was particularly important because it motivated them to succeed academically owing primarily to a sense of responsibility to their parents and siblings.

It is noticeable that parents can be successful with their children and considered highly supportive without the traditional kinds of support that are encapsulated by volunteering, even though our schools value such roles. The ability of the child as student to succeed is predicated on the attitudes above, not necessarily the actions treasured by the professional school community. Setting high expectations and providing an environment within which success is valued and supported are the key aspects of a child's success. The implications again for our schools in our relationship with our parents are significant.

What should the Christian school do? We suggest the following five elements, not as prescriptive solutions since the situation is still developing in our schools, but as considerations for conversation and action:

1. Recognize that there are almost certainly issues within the families we serve, irrespective of their outward appearance of confidence, prosperity, and spiritual practices. There are issues. Christian school administrators must be sensitive to the data points from parents demonstrating what the research is saying, students showing stress points, families voicing attitudes that reflect fragility and lack of intimacy, questioning of the school's faith / mission perspective. Easy examples are tracking absences due to (or claimed as) illness, and being ready and willing to see a student's struggles as systemic, not individual.
2. Support spiritual formation not just as a student curricular requirement but as a family support requirement. Think about the ways in which the school can, within its resources, offer families opportunity to develop their corporate spiritual maturity. Know that this cannot appear to be paternalist or from a position of authority. It is a genuine partnership where school and parents cooperate and collaborate to learn from each other. In this way, the school's mission of partnership becomes proactive and two-sided. Easy examples are prayer groups meeting on

a Thursday morning and Bible studies sponsored by the school chaplain.

3. Assume that parents are anxious. While parents love their children as much as parents ever have, they are less certain about how to prepare them for an uncertain future: COVID / Ebola and potential pandemics like them are happening regularly; there is pessimism about whether the U.S. will hold its preeminent position into the future; there is a binary mindset that contributes to a societal lack of empathy; suicides among 10- to 24-year-olds rose 56% between 2007 and 2017 – this is connected to an ongoing opioid epidemic; the rate at which the rich are getting richer is fast outpacing the rest of the population; robotics / automation / machine intelligence is turning the job market upside down; student debt is at the highest levels in the U.S. and Canada. What is our message of hope in the here and now? We are Christian, a resurrection people. What is the message and the data point that offsets the gloom and doom? What is the Christian school representing as light on the hill? What is demonstrating how different you are from the media headlines and the secular dismay? Easy examples are the amazing stories of graduates who are making a difference in and for their communities.

4. Help parents in their parenting. This is connected to and different from point #3. Yes, parents love their children. They are not sure how to parent them. The Christian school has to find ways to help them after the children go home. One of those ways has been experienced by teachers as a result of the COVID distance-learning phenomenon. As teachers are connecting closely and on an individual basis with the family at home – the child as student and the parent as surrogate teacher – they are finding the conversations enriching and rewarding and the parents deeply receptive to advice and counsel. This is now a new normal. Easy examples are the phone call to the family six weeks into the school year to thank the parents for the gift of their

children, and the Saturday morning workshop for fathers (compulsory in at least two schools in our experience).

5. Finally, we are moving, and must move, to a new stage in our relationship to our parents in our Christian schools. We can't go back to the 20th century trifecta of home / church / school. But we must also not stop at the stage that emerged after that of the school as dominant and the family as subservient. This was the stage that included sports practices during the time of the family meal, an ignoring of keeping the Sabbath holy, intruding on family time for 24 hours a day and often for six to seven days a week, a daily routine that was bad education and poor formation. This was the stage that invited parents to pay tuition, volunteer their time, and give to the Annual Fund but did not invite them legitimately to partner. We must move to the stage of true partnership where we re-establish the boundaries between school and family, stop competing as our secular colleagues do, stop chasing the secular gold mines, and return to being truly and counter-culturally Christian. Easy examples are a review of the daily and annual calendar.

We should be true partners with our parents; we should support the Vibrant Household of faith.

Note: we often ignore or don't realize the compulsory nature of schooling. Children attend a school because they have to under severe penalties. This is what happens to children in Ontario, Canada, if they do not attend school:

> 12-15 year olds who regularly skip or refuse to go to school can be charged with truancy. The maximum fine is $1000 and / or up to 1 year of probation time. While on probation, students are required to attend school; and if the student skips school again, they can be sent to jail for up to 30 days. Students who are charged should speak to a lawyer.

In Michigan, the entire family is punished according to a 2015 statute:

> Michigan law requires the Michigan Department of Health and Human Services department to have a policy that cuts off households in the state's Family Independence Program if a child is not meeting school attendance requirement.

These kinds of sanctions exist in every state / province jurisdiction.

The Retention "Plan"

Later in this book we talk about the transition from Admission Director to Family Relationship Manager. Here, we note the importance of the relationship between the school and the family, and note that the Admission Director (aka Family Relationship Manager) and the Principal are responsible for retention as leaders of the community. They cannot "do" retention. That happens at the granular level of one-to-one relationship. They do provide the energy for retention as a topic of conversation. The retention "plan" is connected to and distinct from the enrollment plan:

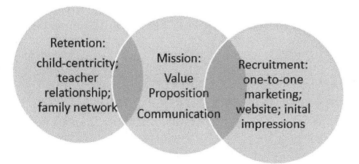

The retention "plan" is a set of attitudes and habits summarized in this list:

1. The school's mission is intrinsic to all aspects of the plan.
2. Every child in the school has an advocate who talks / meets with that child regularly on a formal and informal basis.
3. Every child in the school has a plan for the year that is revisited periodically to ensure it is still working.
4. Every child knows how he or she is doing academically and receives proactive support and encouragement.
5. Every child has an emotional / spiritual life that the community proactively supports and encourages.
6. Every child is challenged to a high standard.

Every child has a right to a balanced life, joy in learning, high academic outcomes, and personal wellness.

Teachers and Re-Enrollment

Teachers are, research and experience say, the most important influence on a child's success. The teacher's relationship to the parent (in younger grades) and the student (in older grades) is the most important influence on re-enrollment. With younger children, parents want to be clear that the teacher really knows and can individually help their child – and provide them good advice as parents while doing so. In face-face-interviews with the parents of high school students, it is not unusual to hear them say that they are personally not that excited by the school but their child will not leave.

These dynamics between the child / teacher / parent mean that the teacher has a crucial role to play in re-enrollment. Of course, teachers universally have no interest in being "marketers." But, like it or not, they cannot "just" teach either. They must accept that their role of communicating the mission-in-action is a critical one to the school's success (and their career!).

Their participation in the school's Christian Professional Learning Community means that they already commit to having the school's mission as its center of action, they recognize the CSM Child

Principle (see Appendix) as a driver of action, and they are committed to success for every child / student within a faculty culture that continuously collaborates, grows, and is accountable for its results. They know that their own continuous growth is key to the child's success, given that top quintile teachers enable students to learn 400% more than bottom quintile teachers! From that base of community and personal / professional growth, their communication with the parent can be secure and based on four major ideas:

1. We are in the relationship / customer service business.

    This is not about pandering to the parent or swaying with the wind. Being in a relationship business means that the teacher takes the responsibility for communication seriously, understanding that the stance must be proactive and positive. In any grade level or class, teachers can:

    •   Make a phone call within six weeks of the beginning of school to tell the parent what a privilege it is to teach their child and describe something wonderful that they have noticed.
    •   Text pictures of children in action and classroom activities on an ad hoc basis.
    •   Ensure that report cards have powerful anecdotes in the narrative sections to illustrate what the child has accomplished.
    •   Avoid surprises – when something is going poorly, proactive communication with the parent is essential to both apprise and to suggest the way forward.

2. We must connect our families to our mission and values.

    Every teacher has to understand that the school's competitive position depends entirely on its mission and the delivery of mission excellence. Therefore, all teachers must first know the mission by heart themselves. A vague articulation is not good enough. The idea that "we all know what the mission is" without being able to say it is wrong.

Our experience is universal that where the mission is known word for word, the community is much clearer about the practical outcomes expected and designed in each classroom. The ability to communicate that mission, its values, and its visible outcomes to parents is parallel to being able to communicate the same to each other. It's important for teachers to:

- Practice saying the mission on a regular basis, e.g., at faculty meetings.
- Divisionally, in departments, in grades, be able to say what the mission looks like in action.
- Clearly articulate what successful mission delivery means in the life of a child.

3. We must understand that the family typically knows nothing about the school.

Parents see the school through the eyes of their children. That has always been true – it is very obviously true today as parents advocate for their children, knowing only (and believing only!) their child's version. Parents' interactions with the school – either at official functions or as volunteers – is simply to support their children. They are, by and large, not there to find out about the school except insofar as it impacts their child. In their interactions with parents, teachers should:

- Always stress the benefits of the school, i.e., not what the child is doing but why it matters.
- Give more detail than they find comfortable; the parent is not able to read between the lines.

- Reinforce your communication. Give parents the same information (especially if you want them to do something) at least five times.
- Avoid relying on the child's backpack as a good way to send messages – even for older students; send reminder texts and include in the weekly school letter.

4. We must recognize that families are largely selfish about their children and not be upset by that reality.

Teachers must have an interest in every child who comes to the school, but they make their decisions to benefit the group, even if it's not perfect for the individual child. Parents don't think that way. They love their own children. It's not that they are not interested in other children; it's that they are only interested in the others once their own children are taken care of. Parents are selfish, and it's okay. Remind teachers to:

- Remember that when parents are yelling, it's because they're scared, not because they dislike you.
- Keep the child at the center of the conversation – it's not about the adults.
- Be proactive about informing parents. Tell them the good and the bad. It's almost all good 99% of the time – and they still want to know.
- Once their child is seen to be doing well, move the parents' focus to every child and thus to becoming a supporter of the mission themselves.

Re-enrollment is almost completely taken care of if teachers are acting on these four main ideas. Note that "marketing" in this context is the communication of:

- what is true,
- in a timely fashion,
- demonstrating unconditional support for the child,

- as a competent professional.

This is what effective teachers do. It just also happens to be the most effective marketing tool.

Teacher Surveys

We want to survey teachers for two reasons: culture and experience.

1. Culture: we actually do want to know what they think about themselves and their colleagues as a culture within the Christian Professional Learning Community. While the individual opinion has some value, the research around stress contagion and human capital spillover makes it clear that how teachers as a group, as a culture, behave is far more important than how any individual person behaves. Of course, from an individual child's point of view, the actions of an individual teacher have enormous impact. And we can say with some confidence that the actions of the teachers as a whole have an impact over time even greater on all children.

   Independent School Management has a useful beginning to many of the questions it asks teachers: *I and my colleagues ...* This approach really interrogates the practices of the group and works to find out where the strengths and weaknesses are in the culture. A strong culture will have strong re-enrollment; a weak one either will not or predicts that it will not. Surveying teachers in this way punches home the importance of community. The CPLC is not just a cute thought but a – maybe the – key factor in the success of each child. Knowing its strength is a key metric.

2. Experience: we want to know whether what the teachers think is the same as what the students experience. It is almost too obvious to say that the experience of teachers

and children is very different. Here are some of the most obvious differences:

- The teacher volunteers to teach; the child is forced to attend school.
- The teacher has a single focus (homeroom, subject); the child must attend to multiple subjects and experiences and is expected to do well in all of them.
- The teacher is an expert; for the child, every class is a novel experience.
- The teacher learns incrementally; the child learns exponentially.
- The teacher controls the classroom; the child is controlled.

At least some of the teacher survey questions should mirror what students are asked. This mirroring allows us to discover how their experiences differ.

The outcomes of teacher surveys are initially to aid teachers in improving instruction and being more effective in their work with children. However, and very importantly, they also provide great insight into expectations for and influences on re-enrollment. Given that teachers are the single most important factor in a child's success in school, re-enrollment is in large part a function of teacher efficacy.

Teacher Retention

Any discussion about retention has to address the issue of teachers. While we have already said that the relationship between child and teacher is the number one in-school influence on academic success and emotional / spiritual satisfaction, that cuts both ways. Where the teacher exhibits a commitment to carry out responsibilities in a mission-appropriate way the child benefits enormously. It is common to go into schools where one or more teachers is not doing this. They may not be very competent intellectually.

They may lack the ability to communicate with parents. They may not be child-centered. They may not even be mission-appropriate. Rarely, they may be toxic.

The classic way for a consultant to find this out is to ask the admission director or Principal casually which classrooms they take tours into. The follow-up is as casual: are there any classrooms you would not take a tour into? The responses are amazing. Without any sense of irony, it is usual for the administrator to note one or two teachers and sometimes more that they would not take a tour into. With a simple question, we can identify at the very least teachers who need to be engaged about their practices.

The opposite is also true. When asked which teacher is a kid magnet, every school identifies two or three teachers who are sought after by children. There are teachers schools identify who actually attract students to their school just by their own excellence. Children identify teachers that they want to be taught by in later grades.

The reality is that the weak teacher has more influence than the excellent teacher within the faculty culture. Why this is, we really don't know. Jesus calls down the Seven Woes in Matthew 23 on the Teachers of the Law and the Pharisees. The teacher is not inevitably a good teacher. It is incumbent on the school leaders to steward their teachers, to provide them with excellent professional development and to help them care for their children in a mission appropriate way.

And if they can't, it is the responsibility of school leaders to let them go, to fire them, to release them. Good retention is not possible where teachers are allowed to infect the culture. Research says that it only takes one in thirty to depress what might otherwise be possible. Excise them and do it quickly. Your children will benefit. Your enrollment will grow. Your excellent teachers will be happier.

The Whys and Wherefores

The Identity of Enrollment: Who Are We?

Can you recite your school's mission statement?

Can your Leadership Team?

Can your faculty?

Can your students?

Can your staff?

Let's start at the top. If you can't recite your school's mission statement, then how can you fill your school? Lewis Carroll, in the mouth of his character Alice, identified the issue:

"Would you tell me, please, which way I ought to go from here?"

"That depends a good deal on where you want to get to."

"I don't much care where –"

"Then it doesn't matter which way you go."

If **you** have no idea who you are as a school, it won't be a surprise if you find it hard to keep students, to recruit students, to raise money, and to inspire your community. Who you are begins with your mission. If you don't like your mission, then change it. But it's the only thing you have that differentiates you from excellent competition around you, from other schools that would love to educate your students and welcome in your families. Knowing your mission and articulating it constantly in a variety of ways infuses the entire community with focused energy, intent, and excitement.

Let's go further down. What about your Leadership Team? If they don't know what the mission is, then they're all going in different directions as well. That's not a question. That's a state-ment. They're good people and their hearts are in the right place and they're committed to their Lord and they all attend church and they are going in a "good" direction. But they're all going in different good directions.

It's one of the reasons there's so much chaos in Christian schools filled with good people. Rallying around the mission – and its much-discussed meaning, not just the words – provides them with a reason to be a team and not a group of individuals. It pro-vides them with a basis for collaborating across professional disci-plines – admission and the Business Office, academic leaders and development, and so on. The idea that "we are all in this together" enables a team to overcome personal differences and professional jealousies. It provokes the team to identify a common destination and work together toward it.

What about your faculty? Most faculty have a vague idea about what the mission is but no real understanding of it. Grace Christian School in Vermont had this issue and determined to address it. The leaders created a new mission, the Board approved it, and now everything is run through the mission's prism: "Our goal at Grace Christian School is to inspire students to live with character, learn with excellence, and love with the hands of Jesus." It's easy to memorize; more importantly, it has real weight for mission direc-tion and mission accountability.

Imagine the questions a faculty member would ask after each class about the students and about herself: was each student inspired by my class? Was my class an excellent lesson? Did each student learn excellently in it? How would I know? Did we love each other in that class with the hands of Jesus? All of a sudden, everyday life has real flavor to it. Without that, the questions are flaccid and fla-vorless – did we cover the curriculum? Was each student present? Was my lesson well-prepared?

These last questions are ones that every teacher in the universe asks – they are basic to being a professional and do not differentiate you from any other group of professionals in the schools nearby. Asking mission questions about professional practice aligns faculty with each other, provides clarity to students, and delivers an inspirational message to parents through your various communication channels.

What about your students? Why do they go to your school? Can they articulate the reason through a mission lens? If not, it's not surprising that they don't talk about you in the local community and to their friends. It's not surprising that they like your school well enough but are not inspired by it. If something else good comes along or their parents decide to move them elsewhere, they're not going to fight it. A school where students know the mission, can articulate it, and relate it to their own daily lives is a school where students won't go anywhere else. They will actually advocate against their own parents to stay. They will consider their school better than any other. They will be proud of their school and talk knowledgeably about their experience. They will attract other students to the school.

And your staff? It's a constant amazement to visit schools and be greeted by a receptionist who clearly doesn't live the mission. Sure, this person is nice enough. But this gatekeeper to the school is too often clearly focused on being efficient, on being an office worker, on doing the paperwork, but not often enough focused on the mission of the school and the relationships that build and inspire.

It is possible to walk through Christian schools and not be greeted by staff. Hotels mandate that their staff, from cleaning to front counter, greet customers as they walk through the corridors. We should do better than hotels! Where staff have taken on the mission personally and professionally, students talk to them as much as to the teachers; visitors to the school feel an instant welcome and invitation; current parents are as ready to greet individual staff members as they are faculty members.

People don't buy an abstraction; people buy the story of the mission.

Marketing your Christian school begins with that story. Take the following steps in the order given:

1. Ensure you know the mission by heart.

2. Ensure that you teach the mission to all school leaders (including the Board), all faculty, and all staff.

3. Ensure you teach the mission to all the students of every age – if it is too long, provide a simple version of it, even reduce it to three words. In the example of Grace above, the three words the school uses are "live, learn, love."

4. Take it to the next level and drive conversations with all groups so that the words are not just memorized but given content. What do they mean? How are they demonstrated? What is our accountability to them? How do we live them in our daily lives? What should be the outcome if we do the mission well?

Mission is the framework for exceptional enrollment. Marketing the Christian school begins with the mission. Knowing, articulating, and illustrating the power of the mission in the lives of children enables you, with integrity, to differentiate yourself in the marketplace. It gives you a story that is powerful, compelling, and invitational. When the school community is imbued with the story of the mission, inspired in its words, and concrete in its application, full enrollment becomes possible.

Whom Do We Seek – Radical Inclusion and Enrollment

Who are we trying to enroll? This is the next most important thing to being all about mission. Once we know who we are, we must know whom we seek. A simple answer is anyone who wants to come. CSM believes that our schools should be intensely inclusive communities. This won't be every school's answer, so let's look at why it is CSM's.

In the book of Acts, chapter 13 begins by providing a list of some of the prophets and teachers in the congregation there:

- Barnabas, a wealthy Cypriotborn Jewish Levite;
- Simeon, called Niger, probably a black African proselyte to Judaism;
- Lucius of Cyrene, probably a GrecoRoman from North Africa;
- Manaen, who had been brought up with Herod the Tetrarch, a Hellenized Jewish aristocrat whose name is the Greek form of the Hebrew "Menahem,"; and
- Saul, a Tarsusborn Jew raised in Jerusalem, otherwise known by the GrecoRoman name Paul.

The early church reflected Jesus' own ministry to all. The push was always to the Jew first (Romans 1:16), then Gentile, and included the rich and the outcast, the well and the sick, the woman and the man, the free and the slave (Galatians 3:28). When the city of God returns to earth, it also reflects the inclusion of "every nation, tribe, people, and language" (Revelation 7:9). Inclusion is a powerful Biblical concept.

Notice that we don't use the word "diverse." That doesn't mean that we think diversity is a poor word. There's a lot the Bible says about the diversity of creation and man who was intended to "fill the earth" (Genesis 1:28). We note too that diversity has a rich research background. The U.S. Department of Education writes:

> A growing body of research shows that diversity in schools and communities can be a powerful lever leading to positive outcomes in school and in life. Racial and socioeconomic diversity benefits communities, schools, and children from all backgrounds. Today's students need to be prepared to succeed with a more diverse and more global workforce than ever before. Research has shown that more diverse organizations make better decisions with better results. The effects of socioeconomic diversity can be especially powerful for students from low-income families, who, historically, often have not had equal access to the resources they need to succeed.[7]

And yet, diversity as it is used in education is not a Christian concept but a secular idea. Diversity is framed as an abstract – homogeneity institutionalizes inequality in our society, heterogeneity supports a new society that gives entrance to the hallways of power for those who are otherwise marginalized.

Education is thus situated as the great equalizer – diversity is the means by which the "other" can become part of the "we." Ethnic, racial, cultural, sexual, economic (etc.) diversity separate humankind into the "haves" and "have-nots"; education will provide an opportunity for those who are not in the dominant culture. This is not a bad thought. It just is not particularly Christian, although Christians can hold it with purpose.

We see this in the language used by schools. Diversity is often framed in terms of a percentage. For example, we are 20% diverse, meaning that although we are very white, our student body has 20% of the other (non-white) in it. Incidentally, this is rarely true of the arbiters of power – administration and teachers! This usage of the word merely emphasizes the nature of the in-group and the dominant culture. And while sometimes an attempt is made, perhaps through literature assignments more reflective of the various cultures around us, there is little real conversation in the school about what it means to be diverse. Indeed, when the topic moves to multi-culturalism, there is often expressed fear by Christian leaders about values and post-modernism. Diversity and the idea of many cultures tends to reverse into a fear of weakening the strength of the dominant culture without truly questioning the dominant culture's own values and (often double) standards.

CSM suggests that diversity, an abstract word, is useful as we dialogue with our secular colleagues, but only insofar as we see it as reflective of the truly Christian words "include" and "inclusion." These latter words are not abstracts, nor are they passive. They suggest something meaningful happening and reflect an energetic direction that the Christian school takes within the context of a lived-out faith. Inclusion has typically been used with special education – the inclusion of physically or learning-disabled children in our classrooms. CSM uses inclusion in a much wider sense.

One school that has embraced this idea is Living Stones Academy in Grand Rapids, Michigan. Its third value is as follows:

Radically Inclusive

> God calls us to something big: to be a community
> where people from all nations, tribes, and tongues
> can learn and worship together.

Jesus was committed to radical inclusion. Jesus lived in an exclusionary society just as we do. The Pharisees and Essenes, for example, were only male and had to dedicate themselves to lives following purity laws. They were easily offended by Jesus, who sat with "tax collectors and sinners" (Mark 2:15). They would have been amazed too at the fact that Jesus chose his own disciples rather than waited for them to come to him (Mark 1:16), and chose people who were generally from poor and poorly educated backgrounds rather than from the social elites. When people came to him who were typically excluded, he reached out to them even, in the case of a leper, touching him before he was healed (Mark 1:41). Jesus wanted all people to come to him so that they could be healed, so that they could turn from a sinful life to one pleasing to God. In fact, Jesus didn't wait for them to come to him but went out to "seek and save the lost" (Luke 19:10). He wants us to do the same (Mark 16:20).

Note here that radical inclusion does not imply that the school has to bend to the will of those included. Jesus certainly didn't. That would be contradictory to an institution that is mission driven. The school calls all to its mission. In the context of each school's mission, children are sought and transformed. Enrollment is not arbitrary – it is highly focused toward mission delivery. This means that radical inclusion is always limited by the school's mission. Not all children's needs can be met by the school, and the school should always be clear about the child who is best suited to the school's mission. This is a limitation, however, and not a good excuse for exclusion on otherwise arbitrary grounds.

Now comes the hard part. We imagine that many schools might say: we are already practicing radical inclusion. If so, we rejoice with you. But let's interrogate what that means by examining typical barriers, for example:

- What if my family can't afford the tuition? This is an obvious barrier – our schools must have tuition as a significant source of revenue, typically the most significant source of revenue – we can't be radically inclusive if we only allow those who can afford our tuition into our schools.

- How do I get to your school if my family does not possess a car, or if the car is already at work by 4:30 a.m.? If it is necessary for my family to handle my transportation, what options are there for me?

- How do I learn if I didn't eat this morning? How do I show up among all the students who have spending money to use at the snack bar when I don't?

- How well will I fit in? Are there other people like me at your school so that I won't stand out? Are there role models who look like me? Confidence doesn't come just from personal attributes and accomplishments but often from connection to someone who mentors and coaches me.

- How many forms do I have to sign in order to get in? And how long and complex are they? And do I really have to understand them all (especially the theological ones) in order to sign with integrity?

- What about the culture I bring with me? Is it a valued treasure, or is it something I have to leave behind at the door as I learn about "your" writings, heritage, customs?

- Where is power situated and are there doors to it that don't require me to be a quarterback, good-looking, or a 4.0 student? Indeed, are there doors that don't require me to be an extrovert, male, or a loud singer in chapel?

- What marks do I have to get in order to be considered, and what does that imply about my background and history?

- What if I can't make it through the door in my wheelchair?

There are, of course, many more – make a list for your own school.

We do not claim that this is easy to do. Each school has to fulfill its own unique mission and maintain standards that are attractive to families. Each school has to balance its budget and honorably pay its employees. It is much easier to say that we are inclusive than to actually live that out. One school, for example, has decided to be radically inclusive through the use of state government vouchers, understanding that if the voucher program goes away, the school will close. Such clear-eyed understanding, acceptance, and embrace of inclusivity is not for every school leader. But it is an example that leads the way.

However, we also would claim that the unwillingness to interrogate the school's barriers to being radically inclusive is wrong. St. Paul faced tough battles for his entire ministry as the early church struggled with the inclusion of the Gentile. St. Peter had to have a vision to begin to change his mental model (Acts 10). There had to be a church council in Jerusalem and even that didn't finish the argument. But Paul makes it clear what Jesus did:

"Therefore, remember that formerly you who are Gentiles by birth and called 'uncircumcised' by those who call themselves 'the circumcision' (which is done in the body by human hands) – remember that at that time you were separate from Christ, excluded from citizenship in Israel and foreigners to the covenants of the promise, without hope and without God in the world. But now in Christ Jesus you who once were far away have been brought near by the blood of Christ. For he himself is our peace, who has made the two groups one and has destroyed the barrier, the dividing wall of hostility, by setting aside in his flesh the law with its commands and regulations. His purpose was to create in himself one new humanity out of the two, thus making peace, and in one body to reconcile both of them to God through the cross, by which he put to death their hostility. He came and preached peace to you who were far away and peace to those who were near. For through him we both have access to the Father by one Spirit. Consequently, you are no longer foreigners and strangers, but fellow citizens with God's people and also members of his household, built on the foundation of the apostles and prophets, with Christ Jesus himself as the chief cornerstone. In him the whole building is joined together and rises to become a holy temple in the Lord. And in him you too are being built together to become a dwelling in which God lives by his Spirit" (Ephesians 2:11-22).

Don't read this as ho-hum. This is an extraordinary counter-cultural message of inclusion, and we are called to replicate it in our own schools.

Being a school is not enough. Being a Christian school means that we should be asking questions that other schools do not have to. We should not be forced to do this by public relations, by a need for students, by legislation or regulation. We should want to do this so that our schools represent the kinds of community (koinonia) that Jesus would want to enter – not the schools of the Pharisees but the schools of the fishermen. It's not about percentages, about the abstract notion of diversity, but about a reaching out to include and welcome, an active stance that makes the Christian school a transforming force within its neighborhoods and cultures.

How Do We Seek – the Three Christian Marketing Distinctives

We know who we are; we know whom we seek. Now we need to know how we seek. This could lead to a highly technical chapter on methods and practices. First, though, we must identify the fundamentals of what we might call Christian enrollment marketing.

Marketing is a comprehensive activity including conducting market research; finding your niche market; knowing your competition; developing marketing strategies; and determining pricing, branding, data collection, budget, goals, and measurement of outcomes. That is, it includes the elements of a good marketing plan. Such descriptors are very helpful, and we should pay attention to them. And such advice could be given to any school, religious or secular.

But what is **Christian** marketing? Is there something about it that makes it specifically Christian? What is key to Christian marketing? Consider the following three Christian distinctives:

1. The first principle is that **Christian marketing is one-to-one marketing.** In secular marketing lingo, this is termed viral marketing (or buzz marketing or word-of-mouth marketing). But long before the advent of the internet, Jesus exemplified and taught one-to-one marketing. St. Mark records that his ministry began with Jesus walking through Galilee, talking with individual people, demonstrating through his actions that his words had integrity, calling his disciples personally to come with him with the result that "News about him spread quickly over the whole region of Galilee" (Mark 1:28). In order to multiply his impact, he sent his disciples out and actually used the incentive of making a difference to recruit them: "Come, follow me," Jesus said, "and I will send you out to fish for people" (Matthew 4:19).

    There are, of course, many marketing / advertising techniques, but the profound integrity of one person sharing his or her experience with another is specifically Christian. And to be a Christian marketer is a high calling. Jesus specifically notes that this one-to-one sharing of the message, the Good News, is motivated by love. "When he saw the crowds, he had compassion on them, because they were harassed and helpless, like sheep without a shepherd. Then he said to his disciples, "The harvest is plentiful but the workers are few. Ask the Lord of the harvest, therefore, to send out workers into his harvest field" (Matthew 9:36-38).

    It is not in the least either demeaning or too strong a phrase to say that our parents are "harassed and helpless, like sheep without a shepherd" as they seek to raise their children well. Our own personal knowledge of parents, buttressed by sociological research, demonstrates clearly the challenges facing parents today in the midst of social and economic changes that have created greater uncertainty about the future than, maybe, at any time in history. Christian education (Proverbs 7:3), and now in the 21st century, the Christian school, has always been a key in answering the challenges of a world where the forces of evil have always been trying to bring darkness instead of light (John 13:27). We market firstly to share the Gospel, not to increase sales. Sales are a byproduct.

Let's apply this directly to the Christian school.

The people who are going to be most profound in Christian one-to-one marketing are the students and the parents. They are the users of the "product." Talking to their friends back home about their experience, they are the "focus groups" that will tell of your success when asked by their pediatrician or realtor or employer/ee, they are the disgruntled "customers" who will share their discontent on the latest social media platform.

St. John notes this latter problem within Jesus' own family where "even his own brothers did not believe him" (John 7:5). The positive power of testimony is demonstrated later in this chapter where Jesus goes up to Jerusalem, the Pharisees send guards to arrest him, and they come back empty-handed because "no-one ever spoke the way this man does" (John 7:46). The testimony of the student and the testimony of the parent is the focus of one-to-one marketing.

This means that the Christian school has to provide both the student and the parent with the confidence and the material with which to testify. The example of Jesus is instructive in this regard. He did not send out the 12 or the 70 without instructing them. But even more interesting is that, even though they walked with him talking along the roads, listened to him preaching to the people, and saw his works, they constantly needed reassurance and repetition of the same message over and over again. St. Matthew records that Jesus was surprised at his disciples: "Do you still not understand? ... How is it you don't understand that I was not talking to you about bread?" (Luke 16:9, 11). He had to lay out everything in the minutest detail and go over it again and again.

So with our students and parents. What seems obvious to you, so obvious that surely everyone can see it, is not at all obvious to your students and parents. If your school is going to be successful, if enrollment is going to grow or be sustained, if your own students are going to re-enroll every year, you have to communicate the good things going on specific to each student / family, as well as the good things that are happening in the school at large. Literally, if you don't provide the insight to the child about what is happening in the child's life, the child is likely not to understand the change and maturing that is happening. If you don't tell the parent with chapter and verse about the way the school's mission is being evidenced in their child's life, it is likely that they won't see it and / or believe it.

However, if the Good News about the child is communicated, they will share that gladly and willingly with all around them. Children will talk to their friends; parents will talk to all they meet. This is borne out in the life of Jesus as well. For example, when the blind man received his sight, analogous to a child growing in Christian character / academic excellence / athletic prowess / artistic skills / charitable thinking and acting, he "followed Jesus, praising God. When all the people saw it, they also praised God" (Luke 18:43).

This principle of one-to-one marketing cannot be overstressed.

- "Teach" the student and the parent about the growing and maturing in the child's life – provide them insight so that they can glorify God.

- They will go out and share the Good News with others, and they will continue to want to be in such a school.

- Others will be inspired to come and "see this thing" (Luke 2:15).

2. The second principle of Christian marketing is that the **mission is foundational to all messaging of the Christian school**. We noted this in the first chapter, but it bears repeating in this context as well. Knowing, articulating, and illustrating the power of the mission in the lives of children enables you, with integrity, to differentiate yourself in the marketplace. It gives you a story that is powerful, compelling, and invitational. Our confidence is that, done wisely, God's promise is that the Word will always bear fruit, i.e., families are attracted (often whether Christian or not) to a school with a Christian mission.

Saying that the mission is the message seems obvious. However, our experience is that Christian schools can become distracted and pay too much attention to their competitors and to the marketplace itself, and even become forgetful about their own purpose. It is not unusual to ask a room full of Christian educators and administrative staff to write out or say their mission and discover that only two or three people (and sometimes no one!) can do that.

Where that is true, the message is diffuse and lacks power. When we are told, "Oh, everyone here is on the same page even if they don't know the actual words," we are highly skeptical and have never to this point found it to be true. Each school can only do **some** things to a level of excellence. The mission identifies what those are. Excellence is saleable. If your school looks and sounds like every other school, it has nothing to sell and will close. Trying to beat your competitors using their words, their tactics, their programs is a route to failure. You should only do what you do best. Ironically, our secular competition is paying greater attention to this than we are!

Marketing with the mission in mind means paying attention to the following practical aspects:

- embedding the mission on all the website landing pages
- ensuring everyone knows and can say the actual words of the mission along with the school's key values
- ensuring each person at the school has and has practiced their elevator speech to say when asked the question: would you tell me about your school?
  o 30 seconds long
  o first person and active voice
  o mission reference included
  o a testimony about mission impact in the life of a child included
- developing a list of key words that are used consistently and persistently in all communications – verbal, written, and digital

3. The third principle of Christian marketing is that **it comes from the whole school community, not just from a marketing professional** in a separate department. The whole community is engaged in identifying and sharing the message. This whole-community enterprise gives the Christian school enormous respect in the marketplace precisely because it comes from the heart. It is implicit in the first two principles, but it bears saying separately. It is hard to find a teacher who likes the idea of "marketing" the school. Marketing has many negative connotations – the prevalence of spam, pressure tactics to buy, doubts about the motives of the marketer, feelings of disrespect, the feeling of being bombarded. On the other hand, people also want marketing – it provides information about something they **do** want, it provides them with a simple way

to begin shopping around, it surprises with options they hadn't considered.

With the latter points in mind, it means that the teacher or the administrator or the janitor or the bookkeeper can embrace the role of "marketer" and see it as joyful and constructive:

- I am sharing what is true – I have integrity.
- I am sharing something that is very important – it can change your child's life both here and for eternity.
- I am going to ensure that we are a good fit – there are many schools and I have your best interests at heart.
- I am telling you what I personally know – I am authentic.

Irrespective of the size of school you are in, these three principles can be put into effect, and the budget required is very small. Success in enrollment does NOT rely on how much money you have for marketing. It depends firstly and mostly on the advocacy of those who are closest to the school – your children, your parents, your volunteers, and your employees.

Enrollment Is about Invitation and Welcome

Who leads the effort? We know who we are; we know whom we seek; we know how we seek. Who leads this effort is obviously a key person. Typically, this person has been called the Admission Director. In smaller schools, this is often not a full-time person but a "function" carried out by the Principal, assisted by the school's receptionist. We would like to suggest that this person / function is now operating in a very different context and needs to be seen in a very different way.

Vocabulary matters. Words communicate surface meanings as well as underlying values and contexts. In the 20th century, the Admission Director was aptly named. The job was explicit: bring children into the school. This was a technical and not very arduous task. The family went to the church; the church had a school; the children went to the school. Once the child was enrolled, that student didn't leave until graduation unless the family moved too far away for the child to attend. The context of the admission environment included:

	20th Century	21st Century
Church	vibrant life	
Family	stable and integrated into church life and faith	
Child	comfortable within a cocoon culture	
School	the lesser / complementary partner to the family and church	
Education	singular form and outcome	
Enrollment	assumed and for the entirety of the school's grade span	
Society	complex but largely on the "outside"	
Work / career	predictable and hierarchical	
Adolescence	ages 13 – 18	
Greatest stress	the threat of nuclear war and unemployment	
Disposable income	growing but limited	
Color	Caucasian	
Leadership	Authoritative	
Authority	Respected	

These are, of course, generalizations with many outliers. However, they are true enough to help us understand that the job of the Admission Director was more of a shepherding process than an invitational process. The constituent was already there and had only to be incorporated in a school that was an integral part of the constituent's culture. The Christian school literally "admitted" the child. There were few restrictions on entrance and, until closer to the turn of the century, there was no entrance testing, educational or psychological; no shadow days; no fancy admission packets. The family came and was admitted. It was simple and largely expected.

The evidence of that is still with us as we look at how our Christian schools approach the admission process even now as we move deeper into the 21st century.

- Many schools still don't have a person responsible for admission; many schools do but often still think of that person as a gatekeeper.
- Websites routinely expect the parent / family to approach the school rather than the reverse.
- Admission pages on the website are perfunctory, providing minimal and bureaucratic information.
- Use of social media is still in its infancy for many schools.
- School materials are still full of technical educational language.

And it's not working well. We recommend two directions:

1. Each school now needs to have a person whose prime focus is "admission."
2. That person should be called the Family Relationship Manager.

Let's take the table above and put in the 21st century comparison. Again, these are generalities but they are close enough to be helpful.

	20th Century	21st Century
Church	vibrant life	not as successful as the school / often in decline / greying
Family	stable and integrated into church life and faith	connected more to the school than the church / fragile
Child	comfortable within a cocoon culture	sometimes lacking family intimacy / unsure of meaning and purpose
School	the lesser / complementary partner to the family and church	the stabilizer for the family / the "competitor" to the church
Education	singular form and outcome	evolving pedagogies, methodologies, and curricula
Enrollment	assumed and for the entirety of the school's grade span	a choice, and a year at a time
The larger society	complex but largely on the "outside"	complex and very influential on the family and child
Work / career	predictable and hierarchical	volatile, uncertain, complex, ambiguous
Adolescence	ages 13 – 18	ages 10 – 25
Greatest stress	the threat of nuclear war and unemployment	international / domestic terrorism, climate change, and loneliness
Disposable income	growing but limited	significant disposable income
School economics	supported by church and "cheap" in tuition and compensation	autonomous and competing with the society around it
Generation	Great, Boomer, Xer	Great, Boomer, Xer, Millennial, iGen
Color	white (Caucasian?)	diverse
Leadership	authoritative	collaborative
Authority	respected	skeptical of institutions and their leaders

The Family Relationship Manager has a very different task from the Admission Director. In our current context, the school must understand that everything has changed, nothing can be taken for granted, and the process is not an event (the date of entry) but a process (the journey to, through, and beyond the school). The following list summarizes what is included in this process:

- Make the school visible to a potential family that is looking for a school through its relationships (trusted sources of information) and technology (researching your school online) – this family is invisible until it chooses to make itself visible.

- Use internal / word-of-mouth marketing to promote the school through current parents, students, faculty, and staff.
- Invite and welcome families throughout the period of connection and admission.
- Educate the family to ensure mission alignment.
- Deepen the engagement between admission and actual arrival.
- Message the impact of mission delivery in the life of the child on a consistent basis on arrival and throughout the child's engagement with the school.
- Provide a warm experience for the entire family in all interactions with the school.
- Focus on re-recruitment of the child each year – specifically identifying the value proposition.
- Move the family from a transactional stance (I pay for a product) to a mission stance (this school is good for my child and for all children) that is based on thinking of the parents and children as members of a community.
- In either stance, ensure that each year's tuition is not just presented but "marketed" to the family.
- Develop the family's commitment beyond tuition to volunteerism and philanthropy.
- Support the family as it plans for next-level education / career.
- Maintain contact with both student and parent(s) after graduation.
- Deal with conflict with the family at any time during any part of this relationship management; the family is seen as the school's client.

This move from event to relationship management, from a brief calendar moment of three months to the entire span of a family's membership in the school community, from an assumed commitment to an earned commitment, all speak to the need for a change from Admission Director to Family Relationship Manager. And this relationship is no longer just with the 20th century parent but with the entire 21st century family, where the child is an integral part of decision making and parents think of the school as their friendship network. The Family Relationship Manager takes enrollment to a new, more proactive, and highly invitational place.

Prove that It Works – Three Demonstrations of Excellence

Often, families come to our schools because of school families or students that they meet. Sometimes they are drawn to our schools because of our alumni. But how do you prove your school works? Our websites must say not only what we do but what the outcome is going to be. They should answer the marketing question "Why?"

"Why" is a good biblical word – it appears over 500 times in Scripture. Why should you come to our school? It's a valid question. And we should know. Of course, as Christian schools we believe that, for each student, we are laying the foundations of their future lives! "By the grace God has given me, I laid a foundation as a wise builder, and someone else is building on it. But each one should build with care" (1 Cor. 3:10). We are building a foundation for living and for life. We know anecdotally how powerful that is.

Which suggests that we should know and be telling about the outcome. We should be able to say to the family: your child will, by the grace of God, look like this. We should be able to say to the child, you are going to be part of a tradition, following graduates like yourself, and here's what they are accomplishing. We should be able to point to graduates from our schools who have particular characteristics and live their lives in a particular way and who attribute that, at least in part, to the foundation laid at their Christian school. In our faith, we talk about the outcome, the "promised eternal inheritance" (Hebrews 9:15). What do we have as an outcome for our education?

CSM has talked with parents who said that their first contact with the school was through an employee who was so good they had to find out where that person was educated. The story that emerges is certainly about college / university, but almost always ends with "I couldn't have accomplished what I have done without the Christian school and the teachers there who helped me in my journey." Can we take those kinds of anecdotes and turn them into trusted testimony?

The early church was very aware that anecdote was not enough. There had to be substantial proof of what people were saying. St. Peter said: "God has raised this Jesus to life, and we are all witnesses of it" (Acts 2:32). These witnesses were not even just the 11 disciples. St. Paul says that over 500 were witnesses of Jesus' resurrection (1 Corinthians 15:5-8). Do we know 500 of our graduates?

Three Demonstrations of Excellence

Here are three demonstrations of excellence that each school should consider providing. Of course, one or the other may not fit your context. In that case, use these demonstrations to spur your own thinking and conversation to create. At the end of the day, however you do it, you must be able to demonstrate that your school is excellent **through** the lives of children who were educated by you.

1. Graduate Demonstration of Excellence (definition)

- On the "About" drop down on your website, add two categories: Graduate Characteristics and Graduate Accomplishments
  - o Graduate Characteristics: Engage in a process whereby, starting with the school's mission, you identify what you expect every faculty member to be working toward for and with your students.

Legacy Christian Academy in Minnesota encapsulates this in these clear five outcomes, each with a compelling descriptor: spiritually alive, emotionally aware, socially engaged, intellectually prepared, physically active. The school went a step further to create a Profile of a Legacy Graduate:

§ Biblically grounded; disciples of Christ
§ God-glorifying; spirit-led worshippers
§ Intellectually prepared; accomplished learners
§ Morally disciplined; students of character
§ Faithful and courageous; servant leaders

Whether you go the extra step or not, the exercise provides concrete examples of what the school's mission looks like when it is successful. It focuses every adult's attention on the things that really matter, that must happen, in the classroom, in the theater, on the playing fields, in the corridors, and out in the world.

o Graduate Accomplishments: The typical list of accomplishments on our websites (if we have any at all) include SAT scores, ERB averages, colleges / universities our students have attended. That was fine back in the 1970s when a far lower percentage of 18-to 24-year-olds went to university (3.4% in 1950 rising to 25.7% in 1970 to 41.2% in 2016). And it is still wise to acknowledge these measures, if only for public relations purposes. Today, we have to go further. Follow your graduates / maintain contact with your graduates longer and collect these data points (you may choose a different mix – ensure it is a mix!):

• Colleges / universities attended
• Finished within six years (at flagship universities only 36% achieve graduation within six years)

- Independent – not living at home (as of 2016, 33% of 25 – 29-year-olds live at home, higher than at any time since 1880)
- Married (by 30 only 51% are married as of 2019 compared with 89% in 1975)
- Volunteer work (volunteering has been steadily declining and is now under 25%)
- Member of a church (less than 20% of the population regularly attends church)
- Donor to a charity as well as to their church

These would be powerful kinds of data to report that would certainly grab a parent's attention and put credence to the idea that a Christian school has an impact on the way a graduate will live her or his life.

2. Hero Wall Demonstration of Excellence (demonstration)

- Create a Graduate Hero wall in your school – add two or three pictures each year. Highlight graduates who exemplify your mission and your Graduate Characteristics, and who represent a cross section of your values. Of course, you will highlight extraordinary academic accomplishment, athletes who play in the major leagues, thespians now on Broadway, highly successful business people. But you will also and equally highlight the school's values in what may be considered even more important: families who have been together for over 25 years, those in Christian service, graduates who have served the school in significant ways, owners of businesses that give back to the community.

We might think of the first list as being accomplishments that are inward looking – what I achieved for myself. The second list recognizes accomplishments that are outward looking – what I achieved for others.

Your Hero Wall won't separate them out in this way and both are equally important. Jesus told us to love others in the same way as we loved ourselves. There is a relationship between being personally successful in a way that supports me in looking to others. It will be clear, though, that the school's values are far more than worldly success. Such a demonstration of excellence is inspiring to current students and their families, and is also a compelling reminder to potential students / families and to donors of what impact the school is having.

3. Alumni Community Demonstration of Excellence (application)

It is notoriously difficult to maintain contact with alumni given their constant changes of address. If they don't have a sense of community, they will not feel it important to maintain contact and will quickly drop out of sight. At the same time, many schools find that alumni come back to visit a favorite teacher or attend a notable event – and they want to stay in touch.

Develop an alumni contact point. Even if you have few resources, it is still possible to find volunteers (recent graduates are a good source) to set up a place to connect on social media. Make it a non-threatening place where they can exchange stories and develop their own influence network. St. John's School of Alberta, Canada, now closed, still has a strong social media network and reunions that attract many graduates. If a school that is closed can have that kind of community, your own school has a very high chance of success! Be aware that all reminiscences will not be positive. Our lives are complex, and our stories will be as well.

Certainly, the school's ability to support its alumni has enormous rewards. Norfolk Academy in Virginia has established strong connections with its alumni in the surrounding business community. Summer internships, casual labor, and serious career employment are all valued outcomes. Of course, the employers (alumni) are also happy since they have access to a labor market that has good values and a strong work ethic.

The value of your current students is demonstrated in the community, the graduate employers will be assured that the school is still committed to excellence, and the students gain a valuable leg up as they discern their futures.

Yet another connector is educating your graduates in philanthropy. Hopefully, the child's experience at your school includes giving back, helping in the community, being a resource to improve the neighborhood. At graduation, students can be asked for their first gift to the school. Ridley College in Ontario, Canada, sets up an endowment for each of its graduating classes that only they can give to. The Class of 2000 might begin small; over time, the funds will dramatically increase. It's another way to connect with students who have left (through graduation, moving from the area, etc.) and bind them to the school. It's the foundation of support for schools over 30 years of age.

These ways of connecting with alumni and graduates (explain the distinction somewhere so it's clear) will also result in generational attendance at your school. We have been to many schools where we meet third- and fourth-generation students, parents, and Board members. The school community is potentially the most important community your current parent has. This viewing of enrollment as generational is very significant.

Carrying out these three demonstrations of excellence (definition, demonstration, application) will go a long way to provide your constituency with confidence about the outcomes your school actually achieves. Paul writes to the church at Corinth: "Now this is our boast: Our conscience testifies that we have conducted ourselves in the world, and especially in our relations with you, with integrity and godly sincerity. We have done so, relying not on worldly wisdom but on God's grace. For we do not write you anything you cannot read or understand. And I hope that, as you have understood us in part, you will come to understand fully that you can boast of us just as we will boast of you in the day of the Lord Jesus" (2 Corinthians 1:12-14). May we be able to provide such convincing proofs of our work in the Lord that others will boast about our schools in the day of the Lord Jesus!

The CSM Enrollment Model: Doing Enrollment

The CSM Enrollment Model

Thinking about potential families and inviting them into the school community requires looking at both sides of the equation – what is the family doing and what should the school be doing?

The Family Point of View

The CSM Enrollment Model illustrates both of these sides. On the one side, the family seeks for a school, investigates, and then decides whether to proceed through the rest of the enrollment process. On the other side, the school has a responsibility to be proactive in the actions it takes in order to serve the family. This chapter will examine the process through the family's eyes (on the left side). A later chapter will discuss the process in terms of the school's responsibility (on the right side).

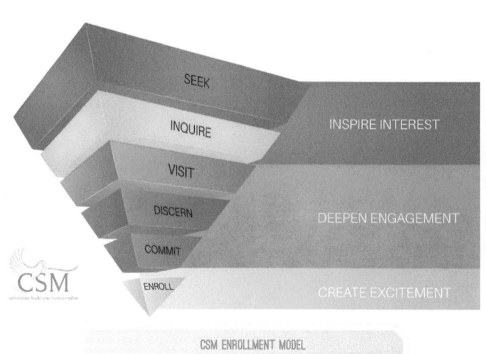

CSM ENROLLMENT MODEL

Enrollment and the Christian School from the Family's Point of View

Seek

Visibility: A family is looking for a school, and yours might be the one. Can you be found? If my family has lived in your area for years, or my family has newly moved into the area, or I'm an adult who has recently had a child and so am newly interested in education, how do I find your school? This is not a question of billboards or messages on buses or ads on TV or radio. There are three areas to be aware of; two are simple and one is complex.

1. Does your school have first-rate signage and curb appeal? CSM has been to Christian schools where even people in the neighborhood didn't know the school existed because there was no sign. Another school we visited looked like a church, so everyone assumed that's what it was. At another, there was no sign indicating where to enter the building.

   What happens if I drive past your location? How does it look? Will I see no weeds, cut lawns, no garbage, a sharp paint job, well-maintained fencing? Is the name of the school clear and easy to read?

   If I don't even know your school exists, that's obviously a problem. But if I drive past (perhaps making a direct physical contact before actually deciding to visit), is that a good or bad experience? It's easy to address issues with the school's appearance, although it can take an investment of time, energy, and sometimes money.

2. Does your school's website come up relatively early in searches for schools in your area, and specifically for Christian schools? It's easy to check! Don't do it yourself, since you may have visited the website recently and the search engine will anticipate your query. Ask a friend who

hasn't visited the site to google instead. If your school is not on the first page, it might as well not exist. This is also simple but not easy to fix. It means ensuring that new content is posted continually, which will keep your website relevant. Content is everything.

3. The complex area is the most important. Do your parents know enough and are they enthusiastic enough to be ambassadors for your school?

- It's important that current parents are well informed – they're the source of most of your new students. You might assume that parents know what is going on just because their children attend your school. Anyone who has been on a fact-finding mission with their eighth-grader about "what happened at school today" knows that is just not true.

- Ask your parents what the mission of the school is or what benefit the school has been to their children. Do they know? Does their response clearly distinguish you from the schools around you?

The child and decision-making: In today's family, the child is part of the decision-making when it comes to schools. Adolescents in particular are involved in the "seek" process and may even be initiating it by talking with their friends and googling websites. They may not be happy with their current school and want a place that will support their academic ambition (it's cool to be smart) as well as their lifestyle comfort (I'm supported in my Christian faith and values). They are seeking a compatible peer group, sometimes simply a place where kids don't swear all the time.

What will prospective students find when they arrive on your website? Is there anything written from the student's point of view and in the student's voice? Are your own students so enthusiastic about the school that they would try to persuade their friends or new arrivals to come? Or be at least willing to share because of their own excellent experience?

It may seem odd to pay so much attention to the opinion of the child. If you're in the boomer generation, you don't think that way. You might even believe that the parent "should" be the one in charge and that the child "should" be obedient. That's not reality today. Pay attention to the interests of the child and your enrollment curve will improve.

Inquire

Each family must find a school for its children. It is a legal requirement. That's good for us! Every family is a potential customer. Every family is not mission appropriate, but every family is available.

Parents want to find a school that will meet their children's needs. Their definition of success determines what education means to that family. Whether the parents are Christian or not, their first interest (after safety) is in a sound academic education, one that empowers their children in leading a successful life. A Christian family will obviously place value on the integration of faith into the children's education. Depending on your admission requirements, you have to determine how to invite families while being clear about your particular qualifications. Clearly, if you require both parents to be born-again Christians with a Bible-believing church home, that needs to be stated. Equally, if you are open to families who value what you have to offer, even if not aligned with your beliefs, that needs to be stated. Recognize that the qualifications you reference will determine whether your pool of potential applicants is broader or narrower; at the same time, by clearly identifying who you are looking for, you avoid wasting the family's (and your own) time.

Families rarely look at just one school anymore. Typically, they will investigate the free public and charter schools, other Christian schools, and sometimes other secular independent schools. You are in a competition. You will not win it by default.

Note that the family is very likely to go through the inquiry phase without you knowing. Just as parents are researching for their visit to the doctor, dentist and lawyer, so they are researching for their visit to you. They will drive past your location, read your website, ask their employers / pediatricians / parents they meet, review your social media pages. You will only know that you made the short list when they actually show up for a visit.

Visit

Parents don't know what to expect on a visit and, not being education experts, they don't know what to look for. They may well have a list of questions – either their own or one they found on the web – that they plan to ask at your school and the others they visit. Primarily though, they are looking for the "feel" of the school and for an "experience."

Who will meet with them? What will be covered and how much has that content been rehearsed? Will they meet another parent who's similar to them in terms of child's grade level or interests or neighborhood? What will the tour include? Have you driven to the school, walked from the car into the building, and then walked the tour route, looking through a potential (and skeptical) parent's eyes? What materials and / or items will you give them? Tours will differ from school to school and culture to culture.

Ask these three key questions about all the steps in your approach:

1. Does the visit speak to community? Your school is a key place where the parents will find friends and have their social circle. They want warmth and invitation.
2. Is it organized and professional? Parents expect high standards and don't want their time wasted.

3. Is it open and transparent? Parents want you to answer all their questions, even the ones they didn't ask but you know they should have.

Finally, don't avoid the cost question. The tuition is what it is. Ask parents about their hopes and dreams for their children, then identify how the school can be a partner in that journey. They are making an investment, even an eternal investment, when they choose your school.

Each child has input into the decision on which school to attend. Even at the Kindergarten level, prospective students are part of the "seek" and "visit" phase.

Age is a key factor in what children want. Younger children's experience centers on the overall atmosphere and the activities and materials they see in the classroom. They also can be impacted by things outside your control – the color of the teacher's hair, for example. Older children and adolescents are more focused on the program, opportunities for them to make choices, evidence that they will be valued, the way students interact with each other.

Control the things you can. Think about your office – if younger children will be coming in, ensure there is child-friendly furniture and décor. Consider soft furniture on the floor, a small bookshelf that they can browse / ransack, and healthy snacks and drinks.

For older children and adolescents, separate these visitors from the parents and have them toured by students who have been exceptionally well trained. Again, keep three things in mind:

1. Student-to-student persuasion is the most powerful and will often directly impact the conversation later between parents and child. It is not unusual for children to get in the car and say, "This is it! We don't have to look at any more schools!" That's your objective. The parents won't go against the child.

2. Find out beforehand, if you can, what the child's interests are and provide a focus on those areas during the tour.
3. Give them something age appropriate to take with them that connects them with the school.

Note: Before the visit, ensure that you and whoever else meets with that child prays for that child. Maybe it's obvious, but the prayer is not for success. The prayer is twofold: that the child might find a home at the school that meets the child's needs; that you will be warm and professional and channel God's grace as you work with the family. You, as the initial point of contact, are going to become that family's closest relationship with the school, if they come.

Discern

If the family has come for a visit, they are definitely ready to commit, according to most Family Relationship Managers. They tell us that if they can get them to the school, they can "seal the deal!" The follow-up is still very important. The family will rarely say yes on the visit itself. The follow-up must be authentic and heart-felt. Consider the following examples avenues of potential follow-up:

-   a hand-written note from the tour guide (parent for the parents and student for the child / adolescent)
-   an invitation to connect on the school's social media page for new parents
-   an email offering to connect them with other parents as well as assurance that they are in the school's prayers as they make this decision

Commit

The family commits and signs the contract. Far more though, it moves from being interested in your school to becoming an actual member of the school community. The experience the parents and students have between making that commitment and the time they actually show up on the first day is an important one.

First, understand that they still have the ability to back out and face minimal or no financial penalty. Maybe it doesn't happen often, but it creates issues in terms of financial planning. You're also not able to make that space available to another family, possibly until the last minute.

Second, understand that from the time they accept, for example, in May until the first day in August or September can be as much as a quarter of a year. That time gives you the opportunity to cement the relationship created during the enrollment process. You want to continue educating parents and students so that they know their roles and responsibilities and can be healthy, contributing members of the school community from day one.

Enroll

When the family comes on the first day, you begin a honeymoon period. In many parent surveys, results show that parent satisfaction is at its highest point during that first year. The first day of school, the first letter home, the first Back-to-School Night, the first report card, the first phone call – all these have to continue to sell the mission of the school; share the personal knowledge the school has of the child's progress; and place a continuous emphasis on the need for parent partnership through prayer, volunteering, giving, and participation.

The CSM Enrollment Model provides a way of thinking about your relationship with prospective families through their eyes. Imagining what it takes to engage them helps the school take a family centered approach that serves these new community members in line with the school's mission, culture, and values.

The School Point of View

Inspire Interest

Thinking about potential families and inviting them into the school community requires looking at both sides of the equation – what is the family doing and what should the school be doing?

The CSM Enrollment Model illustrates both of these sides. On the one side, the family seeks and then proceeds through the rest of the enrollment process. On the other side, the school has a responsibility to be proactive in the actions it takes in order to serve the family. Here, we think about the process in terms of the school's responsibility (on the right side).

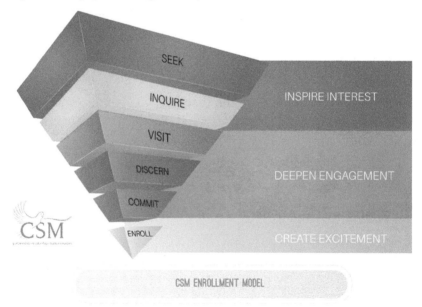

CSM ENROLLMENT MODEL

There are a lot of strategies schools implement to inspire interest: radio spots, highway billboards, ads on the sides of buses, newspaper and magazine quarter pages, floats in parades. CSM advocates that, whether you carry out these other strategies or not, you always begin with a three-pronged focus.

1. Know who you are looking for. Begin your conversations with the school's mission. Look at the school's values. Consider your educational philosophy and the resources available to support it. Very large Christian schools can afford to inspire interest from a wide constituency with significant learning differences because of the personnel they have. Smaller schools with exceptional faculty might be able to do the same. The point here is that inspiring interest from a lot of families that you have no interest in serving or no ability to serve is not a good use of your or their time and leads to disappointment in the community.

   Create a Student Profile that identifies the kinds of students who will thrive in your setting. Don't forget to include a subsection on the student's family – outline clear expectations in terms of involvement, responsibility, faith commitment, character. The Student Profile with the Student Family subsection can be as narrow or as wide as you want. One school we know pretty much accepts any student / family that wants a Christ-centered education. Another school requires a specific faith commitment. Yet another embraces families who want to have a great education, recognizing that the school provides a Biblically integrated approach, but not requiring a faith deposition.

   Obviously, the wider the profile spreads its net, the more potential families can be included. But wide or narrow, laying out with clarity who you are looking for makes you more desirable to those who match your profile.

2. Make sure your website is engaging. Now you have to make that profile come alive. Consider the following as basics in website content curation:
   a. Language that is
      - in the present tense
      - in the active voice

- most commonly has the student as the subject of the sentence
- is concrete

This kind of language provides immediacy, relevancy, and engagement. It is also very hard to do since most copy is written by "academics" who have an academic style – third person, the passive tense, abstract terminology, the adult as the subject.

Academic writing also tends to be lengthy. However, parents and students are not interested in reading paragraph after paragraph of information, especially online. Focus on the key points that are essential to make, and keep the text short. You can get into detail later. Active, engaging, compact language is key to your impact on your website as well as in your admission / marketing materials.

b. Short videos (less than 90 seconds) that illustrate the school's mission and the Student Profile, both deliberately and persuasively. Consider the following approaches:

- Make several videos, each showcasing a single student. Use students from different grades, and ensure that your video library recognizes the diversity in your student body (gender, body type, interests, race / ethnicity, for example) so that potential students watching can imagine themselves in their shoes.
- Tell a story – watch some of the greatest ads every produced and see how in a short time they can create great impact. The story needs to be really simple. Focus on a piece of the mission statement or a school value. Use a visual with a voiceover. Examples might be:

- third-grader leading a worship song (leadership and love of God)
- fifth-grader cleaning a park (stewardship of God's creation and service)
- eighth-grader carrying out a science experiment (academic excellence and fun)
- high schooler chairing a student government meeting (business skills and leadership)

- Make an invitation. End each video in the same way with an invitation to join that student (or one like him or her) on a tour of the school. Or have the final shot be the Family Relationship Manager's name together with a short message (e.g., Join us and experience the power of our mission in person).
- Don't leave your videos just on the website but put them on a YouTube channel, announce them on your social media pages, ask your families to like and share them.

c. Strong images to accompany text. Ensure that the text points clearly to the message of the image around the school's mission, values, educational philosophy (see above for rules about language!).

d. Endorsements of the school from parents and students. Only use quotations if you can attribute them, i.e., include the name of the person. In addition to printed endorsements, consider creating a video using an interview format.

3. Partner with your parents through your faculty. Teachers have an essential role to play in marketing your school – but that isn't what they signed up for. In fact, as academics they may find the term marketing somewhat disreputable. Using the "partnership" lens, you can show them how

important they are in strengthening the link with parents, and how they can do so naturally and effectively. Inspiring interest through your faculty is typically indirect – by enthusing the current parent, they will inspire that parent to share the story of the school.

The faculty are key in inspiring and maintaining interest in your school. Parents trust them; they appreciate the fact that the teachers love their children, work incredibly hard on their behalf, and help them to grow academically and spiritually. Teachers themselves model the mission and values of the school in their own behavior and attitudes. No one has parents' attention like the teacher their child!

So what are we asking faculty to do?

    a. Accept their role in spreading the story of the school to the parents.
    b. Be able to communicate with parents in telling the story of the school.
- o Knowing the difference between features (what happens) and benefits (why it matters in the child's life)
- o Communicating those benefits through newsletters, teacher pages, report cards, etc., in concrete language that always points to the school's mission and values
- o Reinforcing benefits verbally in conversations at drop-off and pick-up, parent nights, in the corridor, at school events
- o Being present with the child in a holistic way from the classroom to the church service to the athletic event and arts performance

When faculty engage in these ways with parents, families have information that they can use to share the school's story, their child's story, out in the community.

Those opportunities are far more frequent than we might imagine: at church, at the pediatrician's office, at gatherings with friends, with new people moving into the neighborhood, and so on. Particularly because you really do have great impact in the life of the child, when other families come into contact with that child and her parents, they are impelled to ask what school the child attends. It is critical at that point that families have something dynamic to share. Their testimony must echo the school's mission, values and the Student Profile. When that happens, the most powerful kind of marketing takes place – the word-of-mouth powerful evidence of an excellent education in action.

Inspiring interest from the school's point of view is the parallel to the prospective family's "seek and inquire." Every family is seeking a great school for their children. When you make your school easy to find and attractive, are clear about who you are looking for, provide engaging information on your website, when current parent and student testimony sparks interest during the inquiry, it is most likely that your school will be placed on the list of those to visit.

Deepen Engagement

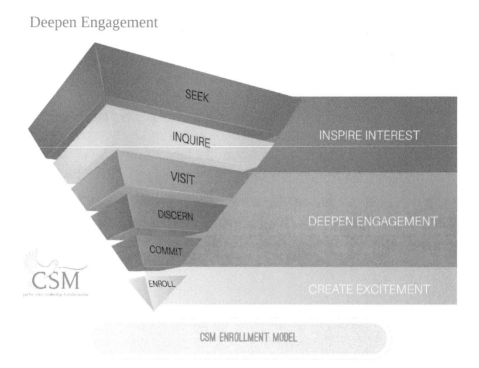

CSM ENROLLMENT MODEL

For most Family Relationship Offices, once the family has decided to visit the school, they believe that they can "close the deal." Nonetheless, let's unpack what that might look like and provide some insights. The family has already indicated that it's predisposed to like your school. Now you have the opportunity to deepen engagement, that is, develop a relationship. The family should have an experience that assures that it's joining a safe, caring, and intellectually thoughtful community.

- Safe: This can have a number of dimensions including, for example,
  - o Cleanliness – Check the bathrooms on the tour route in particular. One school uses the bathrooms to display student art, turning a mundane experience into one that provides insight into student excellence.
  - o Inclusion – Do the teachers engage with the children not only during formal class time but while their

students are at play or involved in more casual activities? Ensure that parents experience teachers who relate well and warmly with their students. Tone of voice and the feel of the class demonstrate your school's commitment to inclusion, with no student marginalized.

o Supervision – Speaking with the parents should include information, told in the form of story, about the way the school deals with child-to-child interactions in class, online, in collaborative work, in after-school care, and in athletics / clubs / leadership programs.

- Caring: In some ways, this is another aspect of safety. Primarily, though, it refers to the student-teacher relationship.

o The type of classroom interactions that occur between teacher and child on a daily basis should be both observed and talked about, with the child's assurance of success through and with the child at the center.

o Talk with parents about levels of intervention when things are not going as well as hoped for through individual help in the classroom; the availability of that same help outside the classroom (helping before and after school or at lunchtime or during free periods for upper school applicants); and the existence, if true for you, of specialists in subject areas as well as support for learning differences.

- The parents want to know that they will also be cared for through clear communication channels, the opportunity to speak directly with a teacher or an administrator, ways to participate in the life of their child through volunteering and / or attending class or all-school events, and the existence of a parent support organization.

- An intellectually thoughtful community: This almost always begins with where your students go to college or High School (if you are a K – 8). It should always develop in the direction of a much deeper understanding of your academic ambition, including:

- the appropriate academic challenge provided each child in the classroom and out of it
- the existence of choice for children from learning centers in Preschool, Kindergarten and Lower School to options and electives at the Middle and Upper School
- the assurance that the student community is focused on academic Middle and Upper School success and thus is an excellent peer group
- examples of individual children who have excelled in a variety of areas
- the 21st century pedagogies that prepare the children for a changing world
- a high-standards curriculum that is interesting to students.
- a high-accountability education that is fun or enjoyable from the student's point of view
- the quality of faculty including experience, education, longevity, awards, and commitment to professional development, with specific examples in each area
- Student led parent conferences that speak to the power of the school's meta-cognitive processes

Caveats

The visit experience is your first opportunity, and a critical moment, to lay the foundation for the relationship you have with these new parents. Some dos and don'ts might include:

- The whole experience must be communicated through the lens of the school's mission and values, using vocabulary that the family will hear over and over again and that reflects the messaging they saw on the website.
- Never make promises that you can't keep – be very honest about who you are, what you can do, who are not, and what you cannot do.
- For older students, ensure the child's experience is very different from their parents', with a student-led tour and

a shadow (half) day so the prospective student gets the fullness of how enjoyable the school is. The more prior understanding of you have of who the child is and where his or her interests lie, the more you can personalize the experience.

- Ensure the parents' responsibilities are also communicated in this visit so they begin to be aware of what membership of this community would entail for them.

The visit is not over until the follow-up has been carried out. The tour guides (parent and child) should send a thank-you email; the Family Relationship Manager / team should send a personally signed thank-you card; the family should be placed on the school's communication distribution list for newsletters and announcements; appropriate invitations to events should be included; a parent ambassador should make a phone call to see if there are insights / questions that they can help with; the weekly parent prayer group should add prospective families to their prayer list.

If the child comes for a shadow day after the visit, a similar follow-up process can be taken with the class the child was in sending a thank you and invitation to attend the school. In this relationship, an appropriate social media connection can also be made. The follow-up process is designed to aid the family in discerning the best decision, seeking the will of God in finding a Christian education.

Create Excitement

Once the family has committed to your school, there's a gap between signing a contract and actually arriving on the first day. This is a time of opportunity to continue the process of bonding the family to the school. Some ideas that schools have used include:

- sending an age-appropriate welcome package to the child
- inviting the child to summer school with coupon for 10% off
- connecting the family with a parent ambassador in the same ZIP code

- inviting the family to school events and providing a free ticket for the child (not the parents!)
- continuing to communicate through monthly e-letters over the summer
- giving them lots of advance notice of the Welcome BBQ that's held a week before school starts
- sending them a survey to discover their interests and talents
- for the youngest children (up to maybe age 6), a 30-minute home visit by the homeroom teacher/s before the beginning of school
- for High School students, creating an event around course choices so that as many as possible can meet the returning students and turn a tedious process into a fun experience

Deepening engagement and creating excitement are all about how the school invites and welcomes families into its community. Whatever you do should be consistent with the culture of your school, immersed in the values of your mission, and aimed always at "connection" in as many ways as possible.

As Christian schools, we understand this process not as marketing ploys but as key ways in which we honor the dignity and value of every human being as a unique creation of God. We genuinely, from the heart, want these wonderful children and loving parents to be part of a bigger community and part of a bigger vision for their family as they follow God's will.

All the actions you take as a school must reflect your own character, your own history, your own culture, and your own faith journey. With each family – parents, child, and any siblings –you are about to embark on a great adventure. The opportunity you offer of a Christ-centered education is a jewel of great price indeed.

The Enrollment Calendar

The Strategic Plan and Enrollment Plan

While we won't go into great detail here, it is important to note that retention and recruitment don't exist in a vacuum. Schools that are successful in enrollment have a coordinated approach to planning that begins with the Board's Strategic Plan. This is reviewed extensively in CSM's *The Christian School Trustee Handbook*. Here, we need to remember that retention and recruitment are not given their foundation in a day but over many months and years of constant stewardship. Caring for teachers and ensuring their excellence in and out of the classroom requires Boards to invest in professional growth and appropriate compensation. Providing facilities that support excellent mission delivery takes capital campaigns, renovations, and construction that the Board plans for and executes. An Enrollment Plan has no long-term chance of success where the Board is not doing its job. The diagram below may be helpful:

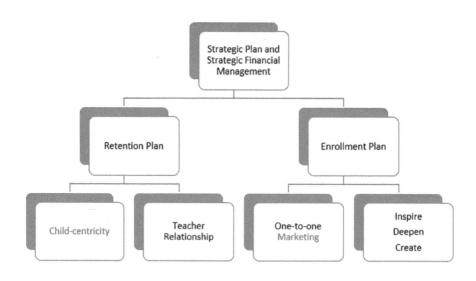

Why and How to Create an Enrollment Calendar

It's interesting to see so much diversity in Christian schools when it comes to the steps in the enrollment process. Here's what we tend to see:

- When Open Houses are scheduled (January to May)
- When re-enrollment forms are due (February to June)
- When new students are accepted (typically on a rolling basis – whenever applicants show up)
- When financial aid requests are due and responses can be expected (November to August)
- When the first tuition payment is made, and subsequent payments are due (March to September)

When we inquire a little more deeply, we usually find that there is only a vague process in place. We recommend creating a document called the Enrollment Calendar, which is part of the school's Enrollment Management Plan. That plan, in turn, is a subset of the school's Marketing Plan, which is a subset of the Strategic Plan, your school's key planning document.

The importance of having a calendar is straightforward. It provides consistency year to year, a framework for action, accountability for execution, and a specific timeline to review. It helps coordinate the efforts of each person / group in the school so that resources and time can be directed to the greatest effect.

Lack of a calendar usually is due to the equal lack of a point person to head up the enrollment effort. For some reason, our schools just don't place priority on bringing students into the school!! At least, this is what school websites often suggest to us. There is no point person, no email front and center to contact that person, let alone a phone and text number.

So our first recommendation is that each school identify the person in charge of enrollment and re-enrollment. If your school is small, it is likely to be the Principal. If the school is larger, you may have a support person who takes the inquiry calls and looks after the applications. Larger schools may have the Family Relationship Manager. It doesn't matter; the key is that someone must be "in charge."

Our second recommendation is that this person convene a group to create the Enrollment Calendar. It should include:

- The enrollment point person
- The Business Manager (or equivalent)
- The Principal (if that person is not the point person)
- The school receptionist
- The development / fundraising person (Director/Associate)

The job of this group is to create the Enrollment Calendar in May for the coming school year. The following outline is not intended to be prescriptive. It will vary according to area and current practice. However, having said that, we commend the dates, events, and timing to your consideration and provide some commentary to show why some dates are better than others.

The Enrollment Calendar (September to January)

September

School has started – you know how many students you have, and the budget has been finalized. Spend this month reviewing the efforts of the previous year.

1. Collect and analyze data (use Excel / Google sheets)
   - Calculate the percent of returning students (not including those who graduated or who moved out of your catchment area). If it was 90% plus, feel good. If it was 95% plus, feel amazing. If it was under 90%, there's work to do.
   - How many new students did you admit? Compare that with your data going back five years. What is the trend for each entry grade level?
2. Review all materials used in the prior year – ask whether each one achieved the desired outcome and whether you have any feedback to back up your "feeling"; compare to see whether an overview of the materials shows a strong brand that is instantly identifiable.
   - letters
   - newsletters
   - tuition letter
   - mass emails
   - annual fund request
   - invitations to events
   - admission materials
   - Review each event in the prior year – ask whether it achieved the desired outcome and whether you have any feedback to back up your "feeling."
   - Open Houses
   - school events the public was invited to
   - special events for parents
   - fundraising events

October

1. Prepare and update materials for the coming season.

2. Survey parents, faculty, and students in fifth grade and above. Without data about your school community, you are flying blind. Know who they are from the inside out. While you can do this yourselves, you are wise to use a third party.
   - Parent surveys are ideally done in October, although other times of the year also work. Never survey parents at the same time you are asking them for tuition, in the first four weeks of school, in December or January, or over the summer.
   - Student surveys are best done between six weeks after school starts and two weeks before Christmas; or from February through May (i.e., not in September or January).
   - Faculty surveys are best done exactly at the same time as the student surveys.
   - Once the results are in, always provide feedback to each constituency in an appropriate format. Include a thank you for filling in the survey and the highlights of the data you received. If there are areas that clearly need work, don't fear providing that feedback as well, appreciating the opinions expressed and noting that collecting both the "good news" and the "bad news" is why surveys are done.

3. The website is for prospective parents and their children. Look at it through those eyes.
   - Go through every page of the admission section and update as needed. Ensure it is REALLY easy to get to a real person. Include email, phone, and text numbers; check to see if your name is a clickthrough to an email form wherever it comes up; put up a picture of the enrollment "team"(Principal, Family Relationship

Manager, academic leaders, school receptionist etc.) with contact information.

- Check every dropdown "home page" and ensure the information is still accurate. This particularly true for the academics section(s).

Make sure that the latest version of the newsletter and any other important parent communications are up. It is not a good advertisement for a prospective parent to look at a newsletter that is two years old.

November

Run your first Early Childhood Education / Preschool Open House. Remember that parents are planning a long way ahead.

Recruit Parent and Student Ambassadors in preparation for doing tours after Christmas. Ensure there is a training process, key language that they are expected to use (e.g., the school's mission), and a handbook, however simple, that outlines the entire process from meeting and greeting to saying goodbye.

Review *your* admission policies with the academic leaders. Check:

- use of testing materials (are they the same; are they in stock)
- criteria for admission for new students
- any students who are likely to be counseled out

If you need to create or update materials, this is the month to get them to the printer. Timelines are always longer than you think, and you always to want to allow time for careful proofreading.

Open the financial aid application process on November 1 for returning and new families, using a third-party application. For returning families, ensure you remind those who received an award the previous year to re-apply. Remind them again before Thanksgiving, when they have time off. Remind them again before

Christmas. Doing this assures your current families that you are taking care of them first.

December

We suggest two letters for the tuition announcement, one to identify the value proposition and one to act as a business letter with the tuition in it. Many schools put these two ideas into one letter – the letter selling the value proposition with the tuition for next year as an attachment or on the back of the sheet. Both seem to work very well.

Write the tuition introduction letter with extraordinary care. Include the following points:

- two or three key school achievements
- referencing the Strategic Plan, key areas that the school is investing in as it moves forward
- classes that were full this year
- the information that the tuition letter will be following within the week

Write the tuition letter also with extraordinary care.

- List the tuitions at the various levels.
- Note the amount per month that the tuition has increased.
- Reference briefly the tuition introduction letter and the direction of the school.
- Set March 1 as the date by which re-enrollment has to be completed in order for the student's place to be guaranteed – new students will be accepted from that point on.

January

Take half of the professional development day immediately after the Christmas holiday (3 hours) to work with the faculty on the recruitment and re-recruitment season ahead. Focus on:

1. Their importance throughout the whole process of recruitment and re-recruitment
2. Their "elevator" speech, i.e., their knowledge of the school's mission and stories to illustrate its power in the lives of current students and alumni of the school
3. The influence they have in the decision of current students
4. The reality that many prospective families will be visiting their classrooms – and to determine a standard protocol when that happens
5. Their responsibility to give feedback to the Admission Office about students' intentions, family's comments, perceptions

Review the tuition introduction letter and send it out over the Head of School or Principal's signature.

One week later, send out the tuition letter with the contract over the Business Manager's signature. Of course, if the school practices continuous enrollment, this step will be unnecessary. Send the financial aid award letter at this time so the family has everything it needs to make a decision.

Reference the letters and the March 1 deadline in all school publications in January and February.

Practice with your Parent and Student Ambassadors. This does not mean that everything is scripted. It does mean that they know exactly what to do, where to go, how much time it should all take, and what information to look for in talking with the family. This is to be professional, to relax these representatives so they can truly advocate for the school, and to ensure a consistent brand. It is not about control. The parents and students are excited to do this work – you want to support them to do the best job possible.

If there are students who are going to be counseled out, that process should begin now. Parents should not hand in a contract only to be told that the school will not accept it.

The First Five Months

These five months are all about reflection, data collection and analysis, and preparation. While there may be some re-enrollment and enrollment activity during this time, particularly with the youngest students, generally the "season" begins after Christmas. Indeed, many schools may have regional agreements as to when they can publicly begin their processes.

The next seven months are hopefully going to be hectic as families return or come for the first time to the school. It is important that you are not inventing on the fly. Have your processes worked out and materials produced so that you can focus completely on the personal side of enrollment – bringing children into the mission of your school, an education surrounded by the love of Jesus.

The Enrollment Calendar (February to August)

February

The first crunch date for your season is approaching – March 1 is the deadline for current parents to guarantee a spot for their children in the coming year. Remember that in January's tuition letter, you highlighted the Board's Strategic Plan, the direction the school was taking, and the general improvements that the school hoped for in the future, in addition to pointing out the improvements that had already happened.

Build on that with your February messaging:

- Where possible, create a sense of urgency by talking about those grade levels that were full at the beginning of the year.
- Be thankful and excited about new families coming to the school for tours.
- Ensure news about the students focuses on the benefits of your education in their lives.

- Profile an excellent teacher who will be continuing at your school in the next year.

Do not say anything that is not true. Obviously. You do not have to exaggerate. Your school is a blessing in the lives of its children. Illustrate that and ensure your parents and the community know about it.

Remember the mantra that parents don't know what's happening in the school, even with their own children, unless you tell them. While secular advertising can sometimes attempt to manipulate, Christian messaging must always have integrity. Speak of what you know and testify to what you have seen (John 3:11). Tell how much God has done for you (Luke 8:39). Be stones and cry out (Luke 19:40).

Make sure a reminder goes out in the last week of February reminding parents of the approaching deadline.

Meanwhile, February is an important month for recruiting new families. Be assiduous in identifying ways to attract them. Schedule active Open Houses where families experience the school. Include tours where the adults are taken around by a school professional and then handed off to a Parent Ambassador volunteer, and the prospective students are taken around (where age appropriate) by a student their own age. Ensure that on these specific days the teachers are doing active learning in their classrooms rather than giving tests.

- Set up neighborhood gatherings. Ask committed parents to host a get-together for their ZIP code. Send an invitation to that neighborhood and ensure families who inquire are pointed to that evening. The format is very simple. Beverages are served. The Principal speaks briefly about the mission of the school, a teacher speaks briefly about the student / teacher relationship, a parent speaks briefly about the school community. Open it up for questions.

Provide a brochure as a takeaway, including an invitation to the next Open House. Have a sign-in to gather names, emails, and phone numbers.

- Publicize school events such as the Lower School Musical or the High School Art Show or the Friday night game and give free tickets to prospective families, inviting families to come and join in the fun. Put ads and notices in the local paper / social media / high-quality regional magazines (whatever is appropriate for your area and your events). Just as a note, never pay for an ad that does not have an invitation in it! Awareness marketing is a waste of money! Many papers have online portals as well where the reader can click through to your website. Ensure there are assigned faculty and students and parents at each event to identify and welcome visitors.

A note about the Family Relationship Manager / Principal: While you may like to have a perfectly balanced life throughout the year, the reality is that you have to take breaks when you can get them because months like February, March, and April are high octane for the person in charge of admission. You must attend all events; be available for families when it is convenient for them to come to the school for visits, including evenings and weekends; and constantly monitor messages. If it doesn't excite you to spend that time in these months bringing families into the community, this is probably not the right job for you.

March

Ensure that there is a a standard thank-you letter with a personalized salutation that goes out to all families who have re-enrolled, thanking them and pointing toward the future. You can never repeat too often the plans of the school, connect to the Board and the Strategic Plan, and build anticipation even about very simple things. Consider these communications as both educational for the families as well as pieces that they can show their friends and neighbors who are asking about good schools.

Re-evaluate your relationships with area feeder schools. Hopefully, you have been developing a connection with schools that end in earlier grades, and they will agree to provide information to their parents about the next-level opportunities your school offers. It is not unusual for a Christian preschool, for example, to allow you to be there at pickup time for the children and talk to any parents that would like to know about next level opportunities at your school.

In the same way, this is now the time to benefit from the relationship you have been building with your local churches. It is unlikely that they will allow you to speak in the services, although some might. They are too concerned about offending families who are committed to the public school. They are not necessarily convinced themselves about the value of Christian education, odd though that might seem. But our experience is that few will object to you setting up a table for fellowship hour and talking to those who want to talk to you. Purchase a professional tablecloth with your logo on it, and a roll-up banner with the same branding. You can obtain these items for less than $1,000, and they immediately projects your image as a professional organization. Ensure the brochures on the table are also well-designed and have been proof-read by at least five different people.

Irrespective of where you are in your re-enrollment and recruiting numbers, find information to push out in your communications on a constant basis. Every week talk about one enrollment number or story that is good to know – we have filled the Kindergarten class and are beginning a waitlist; we only have two spaces left in sixth grade and several applications; there were seven families at our Open House; a Student Ambassador told us this story about a student he took on a tour. Constantly push a story of hope and optimism, even if sometimes, it's hard to feel that way. Each good number is a blessing from God, and we are to be thankful for it. Oddly, hope is the seed for better, even better, results as you move forward.

Set the deadlines for enrollment contracts for returning and new families, and keep them 15 days apart. If, for example, March 1 is your deadline for returning families, March 15 is the first date for new offers to incoming families. If the family has applied for financial aid, the award letter is sent out with the contract. Note that new families that have applied for aid (possibly as early as November) still have to wait until this point in the process before they are actually offered a place. It's key that in the meantime, they are kept in the loop and given plenty of information about the great things that are happening.

Give two weeks from the time of offer to the time of acceptance.

April

Your teacher contracts should be back into you by April at the latest. This is a great time to "brag" about your teachers and interview them about their hopes for the coming year. Publish one interview every month in the email newsletter, or post a video on your website or Facebook page that is less than two minutes, accompanied by a short summary. Knowing that a "favorite" teacher is coming back is a great asset to re-enrollment and some teachers have a reputation that also recruits children (This would also be a great strategy to use year-round.)

At the same time, think carefully about whom you are inviting to return. While a favorite teacher is an asset, a teacher who is known to be a problem by the parent body can decimate enrollment in a particular class. Be courageous and student-centered by ensuring that teacher does not return. This is not a popularity contest – if you know that a teacher is not effective and is not making progress, you must act. We are constantly amazed when we ask admission personnel if there are classrooms they do not include on a tour, the answer is 90% yes! Why have teachers you are unwilling to show off? It's bad for the students and their learning; it's bad for recruitment and re-recruitment. Know too that your poor teachers are no secret – everyone knows. If you are the Principal, ask the tour leaders and Family Relationship Manager once a year if there are classrooms they avoid – remember they are probably in and out of classrooms more than almost any other person on campus.

May

Create excitement about the future. It's important to develop the new relationship with the new families. You'll ensure that they don't forget they are coming and provide them with opportunities to encourage their own network of business and personal colleagues / friends to consider your school for their own children. Some ideas:

- Send an age-appropriate welcome package to the child
- Invite the child to summer school and offer a 10% discount coupon.
- Connect the family with a Parent Ambassador in their ZIP code.
- Invite them to school events and provide them with a free ticket for the family.
- Continue to communicate with them through monthly e-letters over the summer.
- Give them lots of advance notice of the Welcome BBQ scheduled for a week before school starts.
- Send them a survey to discover their interests and talents.
- For the youngest children (up to maybe age 6), offer a 30-minute home visit by the appropriate teacher(s) before the beginning of school.
- For upper school students, create an event around course choices so that as many as possible can meet the returning students and turn a tedious process into a fun experience.

The Summer

If you are full by the summer, this is an opportunity to slow down but not to stop. The three months when the school is out of sight and out of mind can be times when families reconsider the decision they have made. Once a month, send a newsletter that is short, to the point, and encouraging. You might include:

- Key dates
- Links to lists that parents need such as classroom supplies, the uniform supplier, contacts to answer particular questions
- Updates on the progress the school is making (profiles of new teachers hired, the upgraded landscaping, new windows in the fifth-grade classrooms)
- Invitation to contact you with full information – email, phone, text numbers even though you've already given them this in other ways
- Invite parents to host a summer party at their home for new and returning students in their child's grade level. This is a small-group philosophy. Note that the host must be willing for everyone from the grade to come, not just their own child's friends. Parents should stay too and thus see the school as their community. The teachers of a grade level should also be invited so the parents can meet and enjoy the company of the school adults that they will be most closely associated with.

Summer Strategies That Boost Enrollment and Re-Enrollment

Provide services that families are looking for. Consider:

- Daycare for your families – Charge only what it costs, knowing that it is a retention and recruitment tool but charge enough to cover the teacher, supplies, and administrative costs. It provides additional opportunity for one or more of your teachers, brings parents together, and of course deepens a relationship with children.
- A summer Bible program / summer Bible musical / summer Bible fun–for one or more weeks – as with daycare, charge what it costs
- Summer programming – ask your teachers if any would be interested in running a week or more of engaging activity. The options are endless – focus on things that other schools / the Y / the local museum are not doing. Offer it to your own students and their friends. Of course, anyone can come! Often, teachers will do their own recruiting to ensure the program's success.

Consider how you can use the summer events in your area to promote the school. One school set up a booth at a fine arts festival with its own fine arts teachers and displays by the students, and used it as an opportunity to talk with families passing through.

Maintain contact with prospects through phone calls. This is important all the way through the year and particularly in the summer. Never let a lead get away. Phone families on a weekly basis. Don't use text or email. Phone. Until they tell you to go away, they are still a possible family. It's easy to get discouraged, but stay with it. Families can be a little odd in that they sometimes put off decision making, even in this critical area. Give them every opportunity to bring their child to your school.

The Enrollment Calendar is intended to give you a template so that you can work intentionally and with focus on retention and recruitment. This example provides some key ways, though space does not allow exhaustive lists, to engage your own and new families. The outcome of an excellent Enrollment Calendar is that you open in September with more students than you had last September and that well over 90% of your own students returned.

Caveat: This calendar is not intended to be set in stone, as "the CSM way to do this." One Christian school we know only guarantees current family places until the first week in November, for example. There is a lot of variation. However, CSM believes that the elements of the calendar are sound and that enrollment timing should be considered by any Christian school.

The Student Influence on Enrollment

Student Influence: Data

In the 20th century, we paid little attention to the student. Children were an integral part of the family, and the authority of the family was vested in the parents, often the father. As the century progressed, the nature of authority changed and began to be more equally spread, first between the mother and father, and then among the children as well. By the time a family arrives to visit your school, you have to assume that the child has a significant voice in the decision to choose you, and also the decision to stay. There are many exceptions to all these generalities, so the school must discern how the family structure is composed. However, the data is strong around the trend and the following table gives a rough idea as to how it works:

Enrollment and the Child's Influence	
Preschool and Kindergarten Level of influence from 0% to 100%	The child's emotional response to the teacher, to the adults she meets, and in her reaction to being in the class, is a prime influencer. Your recognition of this means that the experience will be carefully structured.
1st to 4th grade Level of influence from 25% to 100%	The child's response to the teacher is a key here. Children tend to still be very open to each other at this age and so the tour guide and the adults in the classroom become a prime influence. When your tour guide "chooses" some classrooms over others, it is a warning about teacher effectiveness!
5th to 8th grade Level of influence from 50% to 100%	The importance of the peer is the prime influence here – will I have a friend and will the other students accept me? The ability of the on-site experience to assure the child that this is a welcoming community (at the peer level) will have a very strong impact. The other prime influence is the ability of the child to have some choice and not be treated like an elementary student.
9th to 12th grade Level of influence is 100% even when it looks as if it isn't – the parent will not go against the child	The young person here is much more clearly focused on "success" as the parent (and sometimes the peer) has defined it. Students want to know whether the teachers will enable their success academically, whether the school has a good reputation in their area of interest (athletics, drama, music, etc.), and whether their peer group is facing in the same direction as they are.

As an example, at one very conservative Christian school, parents were asked the question, "What level of influence did your child have on the decision to attend this school?" The responses were:

	Top 2	Bottom 2	Mean
Child's Influence	18%	67%	2.1

This included children from K – 12.

When the sixth- to 12th-grade students were asked the same question as to how much influence they had in the decision, their responses were:

	6th	7th	8th	9th	10th	11th	12th	6th to 12th
Mean	3.1	3.3	3.1	3.2	3.3	2.4	3.1	3.1

What is striking here is the consistency across grades. It would be normal and appropriate for students at teenage years to be included in the conversation. It is clear that across all demographics, children of all ages are a part of the enrollment (and assuredly re-enrollment) conversations.

Student Influence: On-Site Experience

In a face-to-face interview, one father told the story of his own search for a school for his daughter, a fifth-grade student. The family had recently moved into the area. He and his daughter had a list of five schools to visit on a single day. They had been to the first two schools where, he said, he felt as if he were treated as a checkbook by schools that were very full of themselves. At the third school, his daughter was whisked off to her own tour, and he found himself in an animated conversation with a current parent who was intent on telling everything wonderful about the school that she could. When he got back into his car and his daughter jumped in beside him, she said: "We don't have to visit any more schools, I'm coming here!"

She told her father about the experience she had – arriving at the classroom to find a girl her age waiting outside to introduce her to the class; finding a chair at the front of the class; being peppered with questions about Scotland, the place she had just come from; visiting with the students as they worked; and already connecting with two girls on social media.

This kind of attention to detail from the point of view of the child is very important today. While the parent won't give unfettered choice to the child (you can do what you want) until the high school years, the parent will pay attention to the child because the parent wants the choice to be a success and the child to be happy. Here are some thoughts to consider:

- Pay attention to the application form: What are the child's interests (particularly at the older grades)? If the application form has not been filled out yet, can this basic information be discovered in the first few minutes of the family arriving at the school?
- Will the child meet someone "like" her on the tour? Consider the child's:
  - age
  - gender
  - race
  - address
  - interests
  - friendliness
  - connection to a friend at the school
- Has the tour guide been briefed so that the guide's casual conversation is purposeful and does not hit any minefields?
- Are there any obvious questions that need to be asked by the Principal / Head of School and NOT by the tour guide?

For students at very young ages, have you considered what is happening while "adult" conversation takes place? For example, are there age-appropriate educational toys to play with, appropriately sized soft furnishings to sit on, and healthy snacks? The school needs to show the parent that the school understands how to work with the child, and obviously does not want the parent distracted by the child's becoming bored with nothing to do or irritable because he is hungry.

It is critical not to make assumptions about what will factor into a family's decision to attend your school. For parents, church attended, socioeconomic background, education, and so on may be important – or not. Consider that the child may have a substantial say. This means treating all family members with the respect they deserve. Of course, paying close attention to the child is the right thing to do, whether or not he or she has any decision-making status!

Admission Testing: Support Student Success

Admission testing not only provides the data you need to ensure your ability to make excellent academic decisions. It's also an opportunity to demonstrate the thoughtfulness of your education, your use of appropriate educational research, the care you take of your students, and your desire for the family to have a great experience. As the family goes through what CSM calls the Seek and Inquire part of their enrollment process, you as a school are doing your best to inspire interest. By taking the steps described below, you will encourage the family to take the next steps in enrolling their child.

Almost all schools use three kinds of data to assess a child's academic potential to see if the school can meet the child's needs: testing, prior school report cards, and personal judgment / intuition during the visit. Here we consider only testing.

Testing is not a neutral process – it is not equal for all children in any number of ways:

- Research shows that everybody has a "best time of day," and that that time is idiosyncratic to the individual, i.e., it can be different for each person. Wile and Shouppe reported in a 2011 literature examination that one study "found approximately a six-point difference in Full Scale IQ equivalents between an individual's circadian arousal pattern and time of testing." (p. 23)[8]

- We know that as children enter puberty, their biochronology shifts later. While younger children might bounce into school at 7:30, adolescents can remain bleary-eyed till 11 a.m. An ECS Briefing Paper by Clark and Lee (2014) reported that "students lose as much as an average of 2.7 hours of sleep on school days. This is why sleep loss in adolescence is greater than at any period in our lives."[9] This loss of sleep has innumerable impacts on learning, health, and even car accidents.

- A 2015 study of Danish students and the impact of time-of-day on their testing outcomes is particularly powerful since the researchers (Sievertsen et al., 2015) were able to separate the effect of time from many other possible impacts including socioeconomic status, race, gender, and so on. They found that "for every hour later in the day, test performance decreases by 0.9% of an SD (95% CI, 0.7–1.0%). However, a 20- to 30-minute break improves average test performance by 1.7% of an SD (95% CI, 1.2–2.2%)."[10] Both of these outcomes – positive and negative – are highly significant. They are large enough to impact admission decisions for borderline students. We note that the study was of elementary and early adolescents (grades 2 – 8), not older teenagers.

For an admission visit including a testing component, obviously the school does not have control over the students' academic day. However, to get optimal results that can be trusted, the Family Relationship Manager / Principal can both provide advice to parents as well as set up processes for visits that are as favorable as possible to the child / adolescent. We recommend that the following advice be provided in a letter to prospective families:

- Ensure the child gets good sleep for the week prior to the visit.

- Provide the child with good nutrition prior to the visit.
- Hydrate! Bring a water bottle for the child to use during the visit.
- Give clear reasons for why you make these suggestions, including the school's desire to see the child put her best foot forward. Emphasize that you don't want the child to be disadvantaged merely because of biological realities.
- Include an encouraging note to the child, personalizing it with the child's name, assuring the child that you want the best for him or her.

Sample note to the child:

We are looking forward to your visit to our school! We want you to do your best on your visit because we would love to invite you to be a student here. As a Christian school, we pay great attention to how God made you. So because God invented time, and eating and drinking, and sleeping, all for our health, we suggest that you:

- *Sleep really well before you come.*
- *Drink some water and bring a water bottle.*
- *Eat your favorite (healthy) snack.*

Doing this will help you have a great time and do your best. See you on (date)!!

We recommend that the school do the following:

- Schedule visits for teenagers in the late morning.
- Provide bottled water for visiting students, as needed. For those who brought their own water bottle, offer an opportunity to refill it.
- Provide 15 to 30 minutes before any testing for relaxing / playing, and provide nutrition during that time – a piece of fruit and / or granola bar, for example.

With these steps in place, you can ensure that the prospective student will give you accurate data for your decision-making.

The Use of Student Surveys

With this in mind, it is very important to carry out student surveys every year. They should have two layers – classroom level and strategic level.

Classroom Level

The Measures of Effective Teaching Project (MET 2012) found that "student survey results are predictive of student achievement gains."[11] Further, student feedback was found to be more accurate than classroom observations and student testing in identifying high / poor performing teachers. Whereas adults are fearful that students are highly biased and can't provide differentiated comments, in the MET research it is clear that students are able to give consistent and accurate feedback about teacher efficacy. Maybe this is not surprising given that they experience them day in and day out over period of months, if not years!

Student surveys are, of course, primarily to be used in the context of teacher professional growth, and their prime purpose is to improve the practice of teaching. But as a tertiary benefit, they can provide early warning systems for re-enrollment concerns. We know that the primary influence on a student's progress in all dimensions (intellectual, spiritual, social-emotional, even physical) is the teacher. A poor relationship with the teacher, or a poor outcome because of less than excellent teaching, can be assumed to create enormous risk when it comes to re-enrollment. An excellent relationship with a teacher predicts positive feelings in the student's experience.

Surveys are a double-edged sword. Well done, they can provide incisive and meaningful information that can be used in the school's forward planning and in a teacher's own professional journey. Done poorly, they are little better than a popularity contest and have potentially toxic effect.

Here are examples from the Tripod Survey (as documented in the MET report) to show the kinds of questions that provide useful results.

- My teacher seems to know if something is bothering me.
- My classmates behave the way the teacher wants them to.
- My teacher knows when the class understands.
- In this class, we learn to correct our mistakes.
- I like the way we learn in this class.
- My teacher wants us to share our thoughts.
- The comments I get help me to learn to improve.

CSM itself is developing student survey questions based on an understanding of the student / teacher relationship as being in some fashion a reflection of the believer / God relationship. CSM uses the grace / law and justice / love dichotomy to think about God's character and finds that research illustrates this as a powerful construct.

For example, positive psychology speaks to the idea of learned optimism that comes from environments with high levels of predictability and supportiveness. Environments that lack this result in learned helplessness or the idea that I cannot control my destiny. Carol Dweck has discovered this in her own research, resulting in the parallel concept of mindset. While we don't need affirmation of biblical principles, it is encouraging to see how 21st century models of relationship have moved away from the non-biblical teachings of the 19th / 20th centuries to a model that is much more closely aligned. CSM categories include:

- academic support
- teacher relationship
- spiritual growth

Constructing survey items is a precise art / science. They must have the following characteristics:

- Each item only asks one thing.
- The item is clear in what it asks to the level of student it is asking.
- To avoid cognitive fatigue, there are no more than 25 items (up to half that number for elementary students).
- The items do not use double negatives.
- The items include one reverse-scored item.
- The survey uses a Likert scale with five options (three for elementary students).
- The survey is confidential – answers cannot be traced back to the student. The students' results are reported to the teacher only as a class summary (there must be at least 10 students for results to be reported).
- While teachers will probably oversee the survey in their own classrooms with their own students, the survey itself will be handed out and collected by a student who will put the surveys in a sealed envelope and deliver it to the office.

Again, it is important to stress that surveys are primarily for teacher growth. However, their results will say a lot about student loyalty to the school and thus their likelihood of returning.

Strategic Level

These surveys are typically carried out online through a third party that ensures confidentiality and collects and reports the information. Unlike the classroom-level surveys that are used primarily to improve teacher instructional practices, the strategic-level surveys are intended as satisfaction surveys. These surveys are therefore not specific to a particular teacher but aimed at the student's experience with all teachers. CSM categories include:

- academic performance
- relationships with teachers

- satisfaction
- stress
- spiritual growth

The same rules apply for item construction. The same promise of confidentiality must be made. CSM practice is to include students from grades 5 – 12; online results from younger students are less reliable since the context is much more general. This means that there is a gap in knowledge for the younger students that will need to be filled through the classroom surveys and the typically much stronger parent-teacher interactions in elementary school. There are three additional rules:

1. The survey should be taken on the same day by all the students. In middle / high schools, this can be done during the advisory or chapel period.
2. Students who are not there on that day do not take the survey.
3. To collect trend data, the surveys should be carried out annually.

ISM (isminc.com) research indicates that time of year also impacts survey results, i.e., scores in the fall are higher than in the winter but lower than in the spring. This leads to the observation that surveys should always be taken at the same time of year, preferably as close to the same month / day as possible to account for the impact of programming and seasonal effects.

Because these are strategic-level surveys, some of the questions can also be much more pointed toward retention, e.g.:

- Do you intend to graduate from your current school?
- Do you recommend your school to your friends who don't go?

They can comment on fellow students, e.g.:

- Students at my school are a good influence on me.
- Students at my school try to do their best all the time.

They can also comment on teachers / administrators, e.g.:

- All the adults at my school really want me to succeed.
- All the teachers at my school really know their subjects well.

As you collect strategic-level data over time, the trends will become more and more compelling. A one-time administration of surveys is just a shot in time. Once you have three years of data, the story that emerges will and should influence your planning going forward as you consider your approaches to retention.

The Website and Enrollment

Christian School Marketing – Writing Web Copy

The website is the inbound marketing portal that virtually all prospective parents will visit. It is likely that, before you even know they are out there, your prospective parents have come to your website and those of your competitors to look you over. They will have gained a sense of who you are by the words you use and the images you choose. They will have compared your program, your invitation, your academic offerings, your sports teams, your tuition to your competitors and to their own family values. What they find will determine whether you will ever meet them.

Your current parents no longer visit your website. They are coming to your parent portal or parent app to find the news, current updates, the weekly e-letter, when and where the games are being held. They are checking the school's social media pages for updated pictures and videos. They are checking their texts for immediate information about their child. They are not going to your website.

The 10 CSM Web Copy Rules

1. Write with school's mission and values always in mind.
2. Use the present tense.
3. Use the active voice.
4. As much as possible, make the students the subject of the sentence.
5. Use few dependent clauses.
6. Tell the story; don't rely on abstractions.
7. Focus on what makes you different from your competitors, not what's the same
8. Be redundant and use a key vocabulary list to ensure each page's consistency.
9. Appeal to the child / adolescent as much as the parent (MS / US)
10. Keep text short and let photos, videos, student work, etc., fill in the gaps.

Here is an actual example from a Christian school website titled "About Grade School," that is accompanied by an excellent photo of children.

> In the early grades (K-5), academic emphasis is on reading and writing. Teachers keep in close contact with parents regarding student progress, either via Fast Direct, notes home, or behavior / homework logs. Lower-grade teachers send home a weekly newsletter to let parents know what topics will be taught in class, as well as any test dates, special events, important assignments due, etc.

What are the key messages in this paragraph?

- Reading and writing are important.
- Teachers communicate regularly so parents know what is happening.

Let's apply the 10 rules to it now and, for the sake of the exercise, keep it to the same length (62 words). In real life, we would probably want to lengthen it by a factor of two and add two videos, one of students and one of teachers talking about students.

The positives: present tense and active voice. For improvement: the lack of the student voice, use of abstractions, the "etc.," no explicit connection to the mission.

Here is the school's Mission Statement:

> Believing all children are created and loved by God, XXXXXXX School, together with family and church, provides a quality academic structure to educate children's spirits, minds and bodies in a Christ-centered environment, preparing them as responsible citizens for Christian service and eternal life.

Here is a rewrite that would inspire thinking more deeply about what should go on this page:

About Grade School

We are so glad you are "visiting" our Grade School! Here, every teacher loves every child as a unique creation of God. Every child:

- knows and is known by the teacher

- learns to read and write in a quality academic program

- keeps a reflection / homework log to bring home every day to share with. Let us partner with your family to ensure your child is well prepared for a Christian life! (73 words)

The focus is now on the child. The relationship between teacher, child, and parent is shared. The outcome expected is clear. The connection to mission (and the use of key words such as quality academics, Christian, and life) is explicit. Abstractions are removed. At the end of the page, it is clear what the reader should do.

Let's look at a High School example to see the difference when the primary client is the adolescent, and not the parent. The parent will read over the teen's shoulder. But the invitation must be attractive to the student or the student will not come. Again, this is a real Christian High School page:

Mission Statement: to assist Christian families in equipping students with a Christ-centered education, empowering them to impact the world for the glory of God.

Campus Life: XXX High School is a place where students are challenged. It is a place where students discover their talents, what motivates, and what inspires them. During the high school years, our students make deep connections with their teachers and their peers. They become part of a tight knit community committed to learning and serving God. Our high school curriculum includes everything you would expect in a college preparatory high school–literature and history survey, biology, chemistry, physics, calculus, and language, as well as Advanced Placement, and numerous dual credit college courses. Innovative electives, experiential components, and state-of-the-art technology bring the material to life and motivate students. Smaller classes encourage continual interaction, sharing of ideas, and allow teachers to establish a real rapport with each student. (128 words)

Positives: the use of the present tense and fairly short sentences. For improvement: abstract language, passive voice, addressed to parents with nothing for the student, and lack of any explicit connection to mission.

Again, use the rewrite below to inspire thinking more deeply about what should go on this page. This time, we'll make it a little longer so that you can see what happens as the ideas are developed.

Are you looking for meaning and challenge? We have it here for you! And you can guarantee that you will meet the challenge and find your passions within a supportive and tight-knit community. Everyone who comes here is different; everyone who comes here is committed to learning; everyone who comes here wants everyone else to succeed; everyone who comes here is committed to finding themselves and serving God. What else?

- Oh yeah, you'll get to college too! Choose from a whole bunch of really good courses!
- Find teachers who really go the extra mile with you – they actually like teenagers!
- Get to know the other students in our student activities and in our small classes – everyone is friendly and you're to make one or two close friends!
- You're unique qualities are welcome – it's a safe place to be yourself.

We're innovative, we're passionate, we're going places! You will have an impact on us, and when you graduate, you will have an impact on the world. Please join us. Click here and a Student Ambassador will text you! (173 words)

Your web page is a key part of your inbound marketing efforts. This is where parents and their children will search for you as they move into your area, become unhappy with their current schools, or find and talk to your current students and parents. Examine your website messages and test them with the 10 CSM Web Copy Rules. You'll make your school more attractive and your enrollment efforts more successful.

The Admission Page on Your Website

It's quite remarkable that, in an industry where enrollment is the reason for the school's existence, Christian schools pay so little attention to their admission website pages. We will look at actual current examples of Christian schools from a variety of denominations to see how we can critique our own websites and make simple, non-costly, changes that will significantly increase the impact we can have on our prospective customers – parents and children. At the end of this section, we offer advice and counsel with actions to take related to the various examples.

Here's Example #1:

ABOUT ▼   SCHOOL DETAILS ▼   ACADEMICS ▼   EVENTS ▼   FAST-DIRECT   BLOG   CONTACT

This is the home page menu from a school's website. Note that it doesn't even mention admission or enrollment. It is actually quite hard to find where to go in order to make an application. We must remember that many families are now doing their own research, finding out about you from your website, comparing you with other schools in your area, and applying – before you even know they exist. You must make it easy to navigate to your admission page.

Admissions

Welcome Letter

BC Registration/Enrollment Steps

Timeline

BC "Eagle for a Day" Program

Fall Open House

BC Admissions Test - HSPT

Tuition & Fees

Welcome Video

Academic Scholarship
Oppurtunities

Example #2 is the drop-down menu from the same school's admission page. While this school provides a wealth of information about a variety of different aspects of admission and the admission process, it is very impersonal. It does not provide a face and a way to contact the Admission Team.

In Christian schools – largely not so in secular schools, to our shame and loss – we still have not grasped the fact that we live in an environment where customization and personalization are part of everyday life. Our parents and our children do not want a generic experience but one that they feel is specific to them. Our admission drop-downs still make it feel as if they must come to us, rather than assuring them that we will come to them.

Let's Get Started

Step 1

Plan Your Visit

Complete the form below to schedule a tour of the school. At the time of your visit, your student will have the option to shadow a student in their grade.

Example #3 identifies what the family needs to do. On the one hand, we can compliment the breezy style and simple language. It's easy to comprehend. On the other hand, as with Example #2, it expects the family to do all the work. The school does nothing, offers nothing, does not begin a relationship. The family has to provide its information, email, and "legal" names to an organization it doesn't know whether to trust yet.

This problem is compounded on the "Contact" drop-down where the family has to provide their email but the school doesn't have to provide anything. The attitude here is one of complacency (maybe "it's the Christian family's obligation to send their child to a Christian school") and / or arrogance (maybe "the Christian school is the dominant partner in the relationship") and / or just apathy (maybe "there's a problem?" or "we just don't have time!").

Get In touch

Name

Email

Message

SEND MESSAGE

(317) 788-1587
available from 7:30 - 3:15

Address 7565 Villa Ave, Indianapolis, IN 46203

What's even worse is that the school's phone number, appropriately provided, can only be phoned when most parents are on the way to work or at work – between 7:30 a.m. and 5:15 p.m. And who uses the phone anymore?

It is not surprising that our schools are struggling for students even though children continue to be born in ever increasing numbers, as this table demonstrates.[12]

Number (in millions)	2015	2016	2017	2018	2019	2020	2021	2022
All children	73.6	73.7	73.7	73.8	73.9	74.1	74.3	74.5
Age								
Ages 0–5	24.0	23.9	23.9	24.3	24.5	24.6	24.8	24.9
Ages 6–11	24.7	24.7	24.7	24.5	24.4	24.3	24.4	24.5
Ages 12–17	25.0	25.1	25.1	25.0	25.0	25.2	25.1	25.1

Example #4 shows how so many of our schools lose an opportunity to teach the families about the mission of the school, about the school, about the relationship that the school wants to have with them, right from the beginning of their contact with us. This is the admission home page copy:

XXXXXX Christian School is now enrolling for the 2019-20 school year!

If you'd like to get a look at our school in action, come by and TOUR with us or call us at 831-449-0140 to schedule a visit.

You can download and print application forms below.

In order to process your application, we must receive a complete packet for each child enrolling at XXXXX Christian School. The application packet must include all of the following:

New Students, 1st – 8th Grades

Application for Admission (completely filled in)

Copy of Current Immunization Record

Copies of Previous Year's Report Cards

Student Evaluation/Recommendation Forms Completed by Current Teacher/Principal

Request for Student Records *(completed by office)*

Signed Enrollment Agreement

Signed Curracubby Agreement

Notice what a hard sell it is! The prospective family is considered to be ready to fill in application forms and sign agreements, with words like "must" and "all" sprinkled throughout.

Our websites are still mired in a mindset that families will come to our school and that we just need to welcome them in. We all know that is not true anymore. With simple changes, we can move to a mindset that understands we are the ones who have to go and meet our families, willing to communicate with them in a number of different ways at a time that is convenient to them. So take the following actions.

Advice and Counsel

1. Make sure that you have a clearly visible tab on your home page that says "Admission" (Example #1).

2. Include an admission drop-down titled "Admission Team" (Example #2) with photos and contact information

3. drop-down (Example #3). Take this opportunity to introduce them to the key people in your admission process, including name, photo, email address, and if appropriate, a number to text for each one. Depending on your process, you might include the Principal, Division Directors, Family Relationship Manager, Admission Associate, and, in schools under 300, the Head of School.

4. Include welcoming messages and sentences on all admission web pages that demonstrate (Example #4):
   • You are excited to meet them.
   • You will meet them at their convenience and in the way they prefer.
   • You will trust them with your own information before asking for theirs.

5. Include the mission of the school on the admission home page. That is what admission is all about – you are calling families to the mission of the school.

Remember that nothing suggested here costs you money. It is a matter of editing, changing, rethinking the content on pages that already exist on your own website.

Here's an example from Charlotte Christian School in North Carolina, a school that has incredible competition AND excellent enrollment. This message comes from the admission home page (it has been slightly edited for length). Notice the focus on welcome, mission, and invitation.

> Thank you for your interest in learning more about becoming a Knight. We are honored to share information about Charlotte Christian's tradition of Christ-centered, college preparatory education for students in grades junior kindergarten through grade 12.
>
> **Our mission** is to be a Christ-centered, college preparatory school, equipping and developing students to effectively integrate Biblical truth and learning into their daily lives and to impact the culture for Christ.
>
> The admissions process for each division (**Lower, Middle** and **Upper School**) seeks to get to know your child and family and share how Charlotte Christian School teaches students to impact the culture for Christ while preparing them for the college of their choice. We invite you and your family to **experience the Charlotte Christian School** community by…In Him,

Allycia Brown
Director of Early Education and Lower School
Admissions
(704) 366-5657, ext. 6500

JoAnn Calhoun
Director of Middle and Upper School Admissions
(704) 366-5657, ext. 6501

Changing up your website's admission pages is important; changing up the way you think about the prospective family has even more impact. Think about the website as a metaphor for the experience you want every family, parents and child, to have. When the admission website reflects the school's servant desire to get to know, welcome to the mission, and invite to experience and celebrate, your admission process will gain power and you will improve not only the enrollment experience, but the number of children who want to get into your school.

The Discipline of Enrollment

The Discipline of the "Full" Class: Defining Full Enrollment

At the beginning and at the end of your enrollment cycle, defining full enrollment appropriately is critically important. All the numbers used in this article are taken from existing Christian schools.

Full enrollment in a given section / class is the maximum number of children you want to admit into that section.

"Full" does not mean the actual number of children that you have in a section, or the number of children you will cram in so that you can meet budget, or a range of numbers that you consider "good," for example from 16 – 25. It is a fixed number. Successful enrollment strategies know this number; poor enrollment strategies do not.

The Mission Delivery Argument

Let's look at a data array for a Christian school for age 4 through Grade 8:

2018-19	Current	Sections
TK	25	2
Kindergarten	22	2
1st	30	2
2nd	25	1
3rd	19	1
4th	40	2
5th	37	2
LS Total	198	
6th	27	2
7th	30	2
8th	32	2
MS Total	89	
Total in School	287	18
Efficiency Ratio		16

We can see the following points from this array:

- Class sizes are highly variable from 19 to 40: can this be made more consistent?
- Section sizes are highly variable from 11 to 20: can this be stabilized at the upper end?
- The efficiency ratio of sections to students is 16:1. At an average school tuition of c. $8,500, this is not going to result in a healthy budget – the ratio of students to sections needs to be at least 1:20.

Note: This school does not wish its K and first-grade sections to go over 20 students.

What would have happened if the school had defined a full class and built its budget on that assumption? Look at the following chart, which has been simplified. The first five columns represent the numbers from the above school translated into sections being taught and assuming:

- Each teacher costs $50,000 including benefits.
- Income from the students in each section is at $8,500 a student.

The next five columns have taken the "current" column and used a definition of full class to make a similar calculation. Note that the use of the "current" column as the starting point is not as efficient as a true full class strategy would eventually lead to, i.e., the 30 students in first grade is not an efficient number with a ratio of 15:1.

2018-19	Current	Sections	$ per Teacher	Cost	Tuition 8500	"Full Class"	Sections	$ per Teacher	Cost	Tuition 8500
TK	25	2	$50,000	$100,000	$212,500	25	2	$50,000	$100,000	$212,500
Kindergarten	22	2	$50,000	$100,000	$187,000	20	1	$50,000	$50,000	$170,000
1st	30	2	$50,000	$100,000	$255,000	30	2	$50,000	$100,000	$255,000
2nd	25	1	$50,000	$50,000	$212,500	24	1	$50,000	$50,000	$204,000
3rd	19	1	$50,000	$50,000	$161,500	19	1	$50,000	$50,000	$161,500
4th	40	2	$50,000	$100,000	$340,000	40	2	$50,000	$100,000	$340,000
5th	37	2	$50,000	$100,000	$314,500	37	2	$50,000	$100,000	$314,500
LS Total	198									
6th	27	2	$50,000	$100,000	$229,500	24	1	$50,000	$50,000	$204,000
7th	30	2	$50,000	$100,000	$255,000	24	1	$50,000	$50,000	$204,000
8th	32	2	$50,000	$100,000	$272,000	24	1	$50,000	$50,000	$204,000
MS Total	89									
Total in School	287	18	Total $	$900,000	$2,439,500	267	14	Total $	$700,000	$2,269,500
Efficiency Ratio		16		Difference	$1,539,500	Improvement	$30,000	2%	Difference	$1,569,500

The outcome of moving to a "full" class strategy is that the school has an immediate amount of $30,000 to invest in the school's programs. Twenty students LESS creates a better budget to deliver the mission with excellence. This $30,000 is not an insignificant sum given that most line items in the program section of the budget are typically in the hundreds of dollars ($150 for arts supplies, for example). The vast majority of the program lines could probably be easily doubled with the additional $30,000 income. In the school that we are using as an example, the curriculum and classroom supplies line is $55,763.26. An additional $30,000 would constitute a 54% increase and represent an important increased investment in the lives of children.

In other words, efficiency matters and, when carried out intentionally, matters a lot. A larger school is not necessarily better than a smaller school. And it is not hard to work out where a school could get itself in real trouble by *growing* in the wrong way. For example, four more students admitted to a "full" class of 24 adds $34,000 of income (if all are full pay) but costs a minimum $50,000, an extra classroom space, and other hidden costs.

While education is not inherently efficient in the way that other industries are (it is a "stagnant industry"), what efficiencies there are must be exploited to the fullest. That creates cash flow supporting excellence in and out of the classroom and thus optimal mission delivery.

The Marketplace Value Argument

There is an additional and critical-to-enrollment benefit that we can identify. While the education marketplace is not tuition-sensitive, families do not come and go based on how much you charge, it is still a marketplace subject to supply and demand. Here are three important understandings of that marketplace related to the "full" classroom:

1. When you are not full, and the parents know it, the school has no leverage over them. Consequently, families enroll as late as possible (including on the first day back) and they pay as little as possible until they have to. This might seem highly calculating and even unethical on the part of the parent. But parents, including Christian parents, are fundamentally selfish and make decisions based on the best interests of their own families first, not on the best interests of the school.

2. When you are full, parents follow the rules and do what they need to do in order to re-enroll their children. Another key practice in this process is to identify when returning students have priority in the enrollment process. The letter asking for the families to re-enroll should state that you guarantee a spot until, for example, March 1; after that date, new families will be enrolled and you no longer guarantee a spot. There will always be parents who attempt to game the system and leverage their influence a month later (I forgot, I was on holiday, my car was stolen). Applying the "full" class process, the school must say to that parent, I'm sorry but the class is full. In the marketplace, this increases the value proposition. Notice here that parents will follow the rules only if they believe that the school will actually also follow its own rules. It just takes one or two of those conversations for the entire marketplace to sharpen its focus.

3. When you are full at entry grades, and this becomes known in the marketplace, the next entry place down becomes more desirable. For example, at a K – 12 school where ninth grade is full in March, the marketplace realizes that it is going to be important to consider Middle School as an entry point in order to ensure a High School place. The same is true, for example, of a Preschool where there are sufficient new students to fill Kindergarten – parents apply to the Preschool to ensure for themselves a Kindergarten spot. "Full" is not therefore necessarily throughout the school. It is defined class by class and has impact class by class and division by division.

Even in schools with soft enrollment, the marketing use of the "full" class is an effective strategy. Identify the as-few-as-one class that is full and prominently message that. Of course, if there are two or three or more classes that are full, then the message becomes increasingly powerful. It speaks to the school's value, it says that you are a scarce commodity, it implies a sense of urgency, and maybe most powerfully it speaks to hope – the school is viable and will continue to be here to the next generation. It creates desire.

The Teacher Argument

While this is the shortest section, it is not the least important. The third reason for being disciplined around the "full" class is so that we can support and respect our teachers. Teaching has always been a difficult profession, and today that it is even more true. We ask our teachers to do a lot and we don't always compensate them well for it. They are typically driven by their faith and the school's mission, and it is incumbent on us not to exploit that.

Deciding on what constitutes a "full" class is a mix of four numbers:

1. The social size required for a good education, thought anecdotally to be over 15, i.e., the number at which there is enough diversity of voice, possibility of interaction,

collective intellectual prowess, and common knowledge to inspire high-level learning.

2. The size required by the budget to enable honorable and respectful compensation, a minimum of 20 per class (not an average of 20.)

3. The believability factor of parents who are looking for "small" classes, typically less than 30.

4. The capacity of the teacher to teach, particularly when individualization is taken into account, probably no more than 26.

Note: The only researched small class advantage is in Kindergarten and first grade where it seems that class sizes of 18 – 22 benefit; in grades above, there is no researched difference in student test outcomes irrespective of class size.

Once this number has been established and worked into the definition of "full," it is both supportive and respectful of teachers to hold to that number.

Closing Thoughts

Marketing is not a dirty word, and it helps us understand the way in which people think about education and their families. Where we see marketing as a problematic construct is where the marketing message is untrue. This includes a "little bit" untrue! As Christian schools, we want to be very aware that we believe in the truth. Our marketing message must be completely true. If we say that a class is "full," it must actually be full and not one student away from being full. Too many websites include a message such as "hurry in because there are not many seats left," when the truth is that the school is struggling to fill them. The truth actually matters a lot. And this is true in both directions – don't say "full" is 24 when actually it's 26; don't claim you are full when you only have 23. When families believe what you are saying, then you have power in the marketplace.

Finally, notice that excellent marketing here is a means to very serious ends: excellent mission delivery; a strong, believable value proposition; support and respect for your teachers. It is not an attempt to be prideful in your community or to laud it over parents. It keeps the school's focus on its mission and its people and the ways in which the mission can be delivered and the people served to the greatest extent possible. And when your classrooms are full, then you can decide what the next target should be!

Enrollment and the Blasphemy of the Empty Seat

Blasphemy: insulting, showing contempt, or lack of reverence for God (Meriam-Webster Dictionary)

It is shocking that we talk so little about the empty seats in our schools. It is even more shocking that we don't see them as an urgent call by God to act. In many sectors of the Christian school movement across all denominations, we have given up on the idea that our schools can and should be full. We have given up hope and content ourselves with balancing budgets and talking about Bible-based curriculum. That is blasphemy. It denies the power of our God who is generous, who is a resurrection God, who is a God of all hope. The empty seats in our schools are a clarion call to energetic enrollment and retention strategies based on an excellent education that attracts families and surrounds children with the love of God on a daily basis. This is an urgent need and it is a "now" need.

Here is a data array of a real Christian school with enrollment for one year: 2017 – 18. The top line is the actual enrollment. The second line says what a full class would have looked like. The third line subtracts the second from the first line. The right-hand column provides the totals for each line.

2017 – 18	15	23	16	20	11	10	20	4	11	130
Full	15	20	20	20	20	20	20	20	20	175
Difference	0	3	-4	0	-9	-10	0	-16	-9	-45
Grades	K	1st	2nd	3rd	4th	5th	6th	7th	8th	

We can see that this school, which was balancing its budget and teaching a Bible-centered curriculum, doesn't just have one empty seat; it has 45 empty seats. This is not an unusual situation in our schools. Do your own calculation. This speaks in part to the attitudes of adults who have become comfortable with the status quo rather than enraged that the Satan has conspired against us so successfully. CSM calls on all of us to take note: "Be alert and of sober mind. Your enemy the devil prowls around like a roaring lion looking for someone to devour" (1 Peter 5:8). We are paying too much attention to cultural and other issues and have not noticed that the Satan has sneaked into our schools and is happily sitting in our empty seats. And trying to empty them further.

What must we do?

First, we must count. What is a full class in each grade in your school? How many students do you have in it? Create your own tables in a spreadsheet and fill in the numbers.

20XX – XX										Total seats filled
Full										Total seats when full
Difference										Total empty seats
Grades	K	1st	2nd	3rd	4th	5th	6th	7th	8th	

Second, commit as a staff, faculty, Leadership Team, Board to believe the promises of God and trust in his generosity. CSM said this in the original Cord Principle (see the new Cord Principle in the Appendix):

The Christian school includes three organizational partners who work in service to the school's students:

1. The Board establishes the mission, hires the Head of School, plans for the future, and provides the resources (money and facilities) needed for that plan to succeed.
2. The Administration, led by the Head, determines the vision, carries out the Board's plan, and supports the faculty to success.
3. The faculty serve the children, deliver the mission, and act collaboratively as a professional learning community. The staff support both Administration and faculty by engaging with resources and planning for their effective deployment.

But CSM made an enormous error by not identifying the key need to bring about the kingdom of God by filling all the seats in a school! We were not aware that the rot was so deep in our industry that it was even necessary to say that a full school was pleasing to God! So let us say now that the Cord Principle has as its unsaid premise that all partners play an energetic and unwavering role in ensuring that the school is full and that the Satan is thus defeated and sits in no empty chairs in our school.

Third, find out what brings families to your school and what keeps families at your school. Trust in God is not a substitute for faithful action. David trusted in God and picked up pebbles. God did not sling those stones at the Philistine Goliath – David did. "David said to the Philistine, 'You come against me with sword and spear and javelin, but I come against you in the name of the Lord Almighty, the God of the armies of Israel, whom you have defied. This day the Lord will deliver you into my hands, and I'll strike you down and cut off your head'" (1 Samuel 17). King Saul and his followers were also stuck in the status quo – the odds are too great, the giant is too big, there are too many of them, we don't have enough, we are afraid, we have lost hope. It sounds familiar. But David asks: "Who is this uncircumcised Philistine that he should defy the armies of the living God?" And he steps forward and strikes him down. We too step forward on behalf of the living God. And we must look for the skills and abilities and intuitions and people that he has given us – our pebbles, our sling, our advantageous ground, our youth, our mission, our courage, and our hope. We know the answers to these questions. We are not helpless.

Fourth, create an action plan that takes our knowledge, experience, and resources and puts them into daily tasks that collectively will fill our seats. "The master commended the dishonest manager because he had acted shrewdly. For the people of this world are more shrewd in dealing with their own kind than are the people of the light" (Luke 16:8).

Fifth, execute. "These are the words of him who holds the seven spirits of God and the seven stars. I know your deeds; you have a reputation of being alive, but you are dead. Wake up! Strengthen what remains and is about to die, for I have found your deeds unfinished in the sight of my God" (Revelation 3: 1-2).

It is time for Christian schools of every denomination to hear the Word of God, believe the Word of God, follow the Word of God, and fill the empty seats. Not to do so is to cede those seats to the Satan who rules this world (Ephesians 6:12). He is not our ruler. We serve One who has already defeated the Satan and gives us hope everlasting.

Additional note: The CSM Child Principle (see the Appendix) reminds us who we are serving under God: the child. He came to us in Jesus, a child teaching in the Temple (Luke 2:46) and a man teaching the multitudes. In our schools we must note that God came to Adam and Eve within his creation and Jesus comes to us within the context of our lives. This is our model of how we should approach children – within the context of their own lives, teaching them where they are and in the way they can understand. It is our adult self-centeredness that gets us away from focusing on the child and stops us from being ambitious for God and through God. Instead, we focus on culture or money or capital campaigns, and the lack of child-centeredness undermines everything we do. It stops us focusing on the child and the seats the child is not occupying.

Being child-centered asks us to leave behind our own adult self-ishness (which scripturally is always attached to ambition, cf. 2 Corinthians 12:20; Galatians 5:20; Philippians 2:3; James 3:14). It asks us to come toward the child within the child's own context and in a way that makes sense to the child. This is very different from the world's choice to act as if the child is the center of the universe – the child is center to the universe of the Christian school, because it is expressly the **child**, and **not** the adult that the Christian school is called to serve. Indeed, it asks us to exercise authority in order to serve the child, not to dominate the child.

But all this service is meaningless when we think about the empty seats in our schools.

Enrollment and the Foolishness of the Empty Seat

Beyond the blasphemy of the empty seat, such empty seats are (secondarily) foolish in other ways. Here are seven benefits for each seat you fill:

1. The student adds another set of skills, attitudes, aptitudes, behaviors, and genius to the class and to the school.
2. The student adds to the academic competition within the class.
3. The student adds another possibility for friendship.
4. The student offers one more chance of being excellent in drama, athletics, the debate club, creating the yearbook, and so on.
5. The family is another family in the community talking about the school.
6. The family is another source of gifts to the school, financial, volunteer, Parent Association, room mom, etc.
7. The student represents another tuition.

When a seat remains unfilled, that's a lot of opportunity not available. Let's focus on the last one, just to make the issue dramatic. We'll use the same school data from the "Enrollment and the Blasphemy of the Empty Seat" section:

2017 – 18	15	23	16	20	11	10	20	4	11	130
Full	15	20	20	20	20	20	20	20	20	175
Difference	0	3	-4	0	-9	-10	0	-16	-9	-45
Grades	K	1st	2nd	3rd	4th	5th	6th	7th	8th	

In this school with a total enrollment of 130 students, we can see that three grades are full, one is over-enrolled, and six have seats empty. In a best-case scenario, all classrooms would have 20 students in them. This school had an average $5,500 tuition and provided tuition assistance / financial aid / discounted tuition of an average $1,300 per student, giving a net tuition per student of $4,200. This is the implication:

2017 – 18	15	23	16	20	11	10	20	4	11	130
Full	15	20	20	20	20	20	20	20	20	175
Difference	0	3	-4	0	-9	-10	0	-16	-9	-45
	K	1st	2nd	3rd	4th	5th	6th	7th	8th	
Additional Income	0	-12,600	16,800	0	37,800	42,000	0	67,200	37,800	$189,000
Net Tuition of $4,200	$4,200	$4,200	$4,200	$4,200	$4,200	$42,00	$4,200	$4,200	$4,200	

It is clear that this school, even accounting for lost revenue in first grade by capping the class at 20, could increase its revenue by $189,000, including significant amounts of financial aid. Now let's compare that number to the school's current budget (based on tuition only) and see what impact that would have:

Net Tuition	$4,200
Number of Students	130
Current Total Income	$546,000
Net Tuition	$4,200
Number of Students	175
Potential Income	$735,000
Difference	$189,000

The implication is that this school could increase its revenue by almost 35% just by filling the empty seats. Let's be incredibly conservative and imagine (not necessarily true at all) that we would have to discount seats further and that additional revenue is "only" half that number, i.e., $94,500 – an additional 17%+. What might the school do with that revenue?

This is what Boards would love to do with the funds – reduce tuition! That is exactly what the school must NOT do! Why not? Because at this tuition level, we already know certain fiscal conclusions must be true without knowing anything else about the school:

- The Administration, faculty, and staff are not competitively paid; in fact, it is almost certain that the school is paying its employees wages that will qualify their families for food stamps.
- There is no cash reserve to set aside for the day when the roof needs replacing or there is a significant economic downturn that happens about every 10 – 15 years.
- Classroom resources are stretched to the limit, and faculty are paying for materials out of their own wages.
- Professional development is dependent entirely on Title 1 and Title 2 funds because there is no school budget for them.

Let's imagine that the school has 14 employees – one for each grade, an additional person in K, two specialists, the school secretary and a Principal. CSM says that compensation is between 70% – 80% of the total budget. That would look like this:

80%	$436,800
Employees	14
Average	$31,200

Fixed costs take up three quarters of the rest (utilities, etc.), amounting to $81,900. This leaves $27,300 for classroom resources and programming of every kind including Middle School athletics and transportation.

Rather than reducing tuition, the full classrooms now allow some strategic decisions to be made. The school can improve its compensation, provide money toward a cash reserve, and enhance its programmatic offerings. This is what that might look like in the context of an excellently executed Strategic Plan with Strategic Financial Management:

		Current	Strategic	Cost	Percentage
Employees	14	$31,200	$34,200	$42,000	9.6%
Professional Growth		$0	$10,000	$10,000	
Cash Reserve		$0	$25,000	$25,000	
Program Costs		$27,300	$53,800	$17,500	97.1%
Total Use of $94,500				$94,500	

The outcome of this would be to:

- increase retention of faculty (compensation)
- increase morale of faculty (professional growth)
- improve classroom instruction (program costs and professional development)
- increase student and parent satisfaction (all of the above)
- increase the strategic strength of the school (cash reserve)

This section doesn't deal with the many ways, great and small, in which the school can impact enrollment. However, since we're focusing on the way filling empty seats can have a dramatic impact on the school's competitive and strategic position, we will talk about the way financial aid can be leveraged to improve the number of students in a school.

Let's say immediately that the way to fill schools is NOT to give away seats. That is fiscally unwise and depreciates your brand in the marketplace. However, strategic financial aid is a valid way to energize your enrollment and to support a fully developed marketing / enrollment plan. The enrollment numbers below will work to give us insight into this:

5th	6th	7th	8th	
10	20	4	11	actual
20	20	20	20	desired

Sixth grade is an entry point at this school since that's when Middle School begins in area public schools. The other private schools in the area, including Christian, are all K – 8. Nonetheless, the current parent is definitely thinking about re-enrollment every year and particularly when a change might make sense. Marketing principles tell us that something becomes more desirable when it is harder to get – if sixth grade is full, parents begin to wonder if they shouldn't enroll their children earlier in order to get a Middle School spot. Filling sixth grade becomes a strategic imperative.

But some parents will apply who cannot afford your tuition, who are applying when the financial aid budget has been spent, and who may need more financial aid than your "policies" allow (e.g., up to 60%).

This is the scenario:

- The 10 students from fifth grade will return.
- Six students have applied from other schools and will pay the average $4,200 net tuition
- Four other families have applied. They are mission appropriate, but they don't have the money.

The strategic use of financial aid says that:

- A full seat is far better than an empty one (it is easier to market a full school than an empty one).
- A seat that pays something is revenue that you would not otherwise have obtained.
- Helping families at sixth grade is fiscally possible because you only have to carry them for three years (compared with doing the same at Kindergarten when you have to carry them for nine years).
- You give what it takes to fill the seat, ignoring both policy and financial aid budget.

What is the result fiscally? Without those four students, the grade is only 80% full and the revenue looks like this:

	Returning	New	Strategic	
6th Grade Class	10	6	0	Total Revenue
Tuition Paid	$4,200	$4,200	0	
Revenue	$42,000	$25,200	0	$67,200

With the four students, the class is full (with all the benefits noted at the beginning of the article) and the revenue looks like this, assuming 50% of the usual revenue:

	Returning	New	Strategic	
6th Grade Class	10	6	4	Total Revenue
Tuition Paid	$4,200	$4,200	$4,200	
Revenue	$42,000	$25,200	$8,400	$75,600

Revenue for the class has increased by $8,400, an increase of 12.5%. But now you can state that your entry grade is full.

There is another great benefit to full classes. It is that you can begin to set and actually enforce deadlines for re-enrollment because returning parents no longer have any leverage over you. As you know, now they put off paying as long as possible because they know you will take their check whenever you bring it in. That plays havoc with your planning. The strategically full class now gives you leverage to say to returning parents that they have to make their decisions earlier.

You have also improved that class, thinking about the seven benefits at the beginning of this section, by 25%, improved it academically, socially, competitively, and even spiritually.

The empty seat is folly. The Christian school, over time, must fill high entry grades and, if necessary and only for mission-appropriate families, use financial aid strategically as a lever to do so.

The Parent and Enrollment

Tell the Parents What You Are Doing!

The first principle of Christian marketing is that it is one-to-one marketing. The incentive for being courageous and talking to others about the school is that it makes a difference, something will happen that is good. Telling is motivated by love – the desire to really change the possibilities for the listener, to change the trajectory of a child's journey and sometimes even a family's journey.

What did Jesus do? He was constantly bombarded with questions by people. Let's look at some of those questions because you will recognize them in your vocation as well.

- "Are you the one who is to come, or should we expect someone else?" (Matthew 11:3). Are you the best school for my child or should I go look at all the others in this area?
- "By what authority are you doing these things?" they asked. "And who gave you this authority?" (Matthew 21:23). How many degrees do you have and is your school accredited and where do your faculty come from and are they certified?
- "What do you want with us, Jesus of Nazareth?" (Mark 1:24). Why are you looking at me that way? Why don't you go and bother someone else?
- John sent them to the Lord to ask, "Are you the one who is to come, or should we expect someone else?" (Luke 7:19). Do you have the right theology and the right church background?
- One of the criminals who hung there hurled insults at him: "Aren't you the Messiah? Save yourself and us!" (Luke 23:39). These are the "fun" rhetorical questions! How can you do this or say this when you say you are a Christian school?
- "You are demon-possessed," the crowd answered. "Who is trying to kill you?" (John 7:20). What me? I'm not gossiping about you behind your back. Why would you think that I am not supportive of the school?

- She said, "Sir, if you have carried him away, tell me where you have put him, and I will get him" (John 20:15). Yes, I know that everything has gone well for my child, but what are you going to do for him or her next?
- "Who are you, Lord?" Saul asked. (Acts 9:5). What kind of a school is this?

"In reply, Jesus said" (Luke 10:30). What did Jesus typically say? Compare that to the words that faculty, staff, and Administration say when they are asked about the school. Where do you work? What do you do? Why do you do it? The reality for most people is that they answer the question literally. I work at this school; I teach sixth grade, or I sit in my office all day fixing problems; my school is on Yardland Avenue. That wasn't Jesus' style at all. When he was asked a question, or when he was faced with a crowd, he told a story. Jesus told stories, allegories, parables, metaphors, fiction and non-fiction all combined together, all designed to encourage the listener to enter the Kingdom of Heaven.

You want to market your school successfully? You have to learn how to become a storyteller. In fact, the whole school has to practice storytelling. At a school CSM serves, the faculty were asked to share their elevator speeches. This was before any training had happened. The challenge was: You have 30 seconds or less to share about your school. What would you say? The result was boring, not easy to understand, and certainly not going to lead to further conversation. They tried to explain the philosophy of the school, talked about where the school was.

They were then asked to share a story about a child who had experienced something amazing at their school. The change was radical – they were far more animated, there were some tears, they talked about a real person, the time wasn't long enough.

Jesus told stories intended to engage, make the listener come back for more, teach something important, point the hearer back to himself as the storyteller. It was done so well, people would literally walk around the Sea of Galilee to get back to Jesus.

By and large, people don't want facts because they're not interesting. Don't get me wrong. Facts are critical – God IS the Creator of the Universe; Jesus rose from the dead. But the outcome of those facts is what convicts and makes people act. "Go and do likewise" (Luke 10: 37) is not the reaction to encyclopedic knowledge but to an emotional connection.

Train the entire community using some of the prompts in this section or creating your own. Even in a setting where everyone knows everyone else, there is a hesitancy about talking to each other about things that matter. It's just safer to skate along the top. Challenge the group to recognize that if they can't share with their community, how will they possibly share with the potential parent, the hoped-for donor, the community supporter, people they don't know and have never met before? Practice, practice, practice. At every meeting, ask someone to share a story.

When people ask you what you do, go for the heart. "I do God's work with children. There was a boy named Josiah …" Or about the school: "We've been doing God's work for 33 years. One of our alumnae, Sarah, was telling me at a gathering …" Let people see you and the school in which you lead through the eyes of those you serve. This has the added advantage of taking away the ego. It's no longer about you. The story might not even be about a person you personally taught or advised. It's about the child or child-become-adult. We are in the resurrection business. Let me tell you a story …

Christian Parents Are Fundamentally Selfish – Good!

Because the Christian school is so respectful of the parent and the parent's role, it is difficult to get a sense of the true relationship between the parent and the school. A typical statement is as follows (taken from a real school):

> We believe the Bible establishes the parents as the primary educators of their children. Parents must be the primary teachers of their children in such basic skills and character qualities as listening attentively, giving prompt obedience to authority, showing respect for others, maintaining personal integrity, exercising appropriate self-control and completing all assigned work in a timely and quality manner. While the school can do much in working with the parents to help develop these qualities, they are considered primarily in the realm of parental responsibility, and they must be reasonably present in the children if the home / school partnership is to be successful. We view the role of (the) Christian School as assisting parents by providing an educational program that will reinforce the Christian emphasis of the home as well as providing a formal academic and vocational education from the Preschool through secondary school levels. This is a Biblically rooted partnership, in that the Hebrew words for parents (horim) and for teachers (morim) both pertain to the task of teaching and instruction. Thus, Christian school teachers are seen as coming alongside the parents and working to accomplish the common goals of Christian education.

It is not CSM's desire to either argue with or negate these kinds of statements. We have no alternative Scriptural vision. It is our experience that this is not how it works out in practice. While we may be sorrowful about this, the reality of parents and the school is very different:

- Both parents work.

In Nearly Half of Two-Parent Households, Both Mom and Dad Work Full-Time

% of couples, by work arrangement

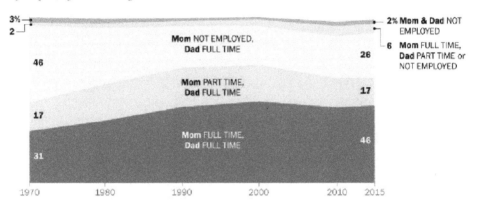

Note: Based on employment status in the prior year among male/female married couples with at least one child younger than 18 in the household. Both married and cohabiting couples included since 2010. Data regarding cohabiting couples unavailable for earlier years. Other work arrangements not shown; same-sex couples are excluded.

Source: Pew Research Center analysis of March Current Population Surveys Integrated Public Use Microdata Series (IPUMS-CPS), 1970-2015

PEW RESEARCH CENTER

- The father doesn't always make more money (in 2011, 15% of households with young children were comprised of a wife who out-earned her husband); generally, each feels equally committed to career.

When Both Parents Work Full Time, Most Say Neither Career Takes Priority

% of parents in households where both parents are employed full time saying ...

Note: Based on respondents who work full time and are married to or living with a partner who works full time and is the parent of at least one of the respondent's children (n=531). "Don't know/Refused" responses not shown.

Source: Pew Research Center survey of parents with children under 18, Sept. 15-Oct. 13, 2015. Q95,96

PEW RESEARCH CENTER

- an increasing number of families are led by a single mother or father

Living arrangements of children: 1960 to present

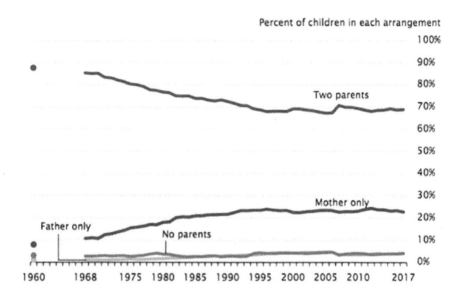

Percent of children in each arrangement

Source: U.S. Census Bureau, Decennial Census, 1960, and Current Population Survey, Annual Social and Economic Supplements, 1968 to 2017.

- An increasing number of children are being born to single mothers.

Percentage of All Births that Were to Unmarried Women, by Race and Hispanic Origin: Selected Years, 1960-2017

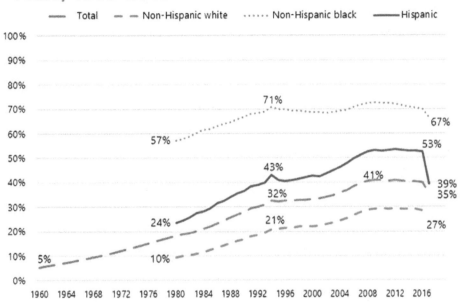

Sources: Data by race and Hispanic origin for 1980-1989: U.S. Department of Health and Human Services, Centers for Disease Control and Prevention, National Center for Health Statistics. (2014). Health, United States, 2013 [Table 5]. Hyattsville, MD: Author. Retrieved from http://www.cdc.gov/nchs/hus/previous.htm#tables. All other data for 1960-1999: Ventura, S.J., & Bachrach, C.A. (2000). Nonmarital childbearing in the United States, 1940-1999 [Table 4]. National Vital Statistics Reports, 48(16). Retrieved from http://www.cdc.gov/nchs/data/nvsr/nvsr48/nvs48_16.pdf. Data for 2000-2006: U.S. Department of Health and Human Services, Centers for Disease Control and Prevention, National Center for Health Statistics. (2002-2009). Births: Final data for 2000-2006. Hyattsville, MD: Author. Retrieved from http://www.cdc.gov/nchs/products/nvsr.htm. Data for 2007-2017: U.S. Department of Health and Human Services, Centers for Disease Control and Prevention, National Center for Health Statistics. (2018). CDC

childtrends.org

These social changes and trends mean that the Christian school must deal with what is, not what might or should be. There is, indeed, a strong historical argument that these are all long-term trends that we have ignored for too long.

The Christian school cannot depend on the family to demonstrate the attitudes, customs, worldview, faith commitment, moral values that the school espouses. In one school we surveyed, fully 28% of the families admitted they never went to church, even though they had to sign a statement of faith and church membership on admittance to the school. Families are split by theologies, political positions, economic strains, dysfunctional relationships.

Not only is the family not the dominant partner, it is not even an equal partner. Whether looking at prosperous families or families in poverty, parents are trying hard (think of your own experience!), working hard, and fearful of the future in an age of headlines such as "Helping Children Cope in the Age of School Shootings." Our schools are locked down (in the United States though not in Canada) and we employ armed guards to walk the corridors. Parents come to help, not to be partners in the education of their children. They expect us to do that job – including morals, attitudes, and the rest. They certainly want the school to reflect their own beliefs and belief / value systems, but the school is where it is going to happen. And by the time the child has become a teenager, in most of our schools most of the time, the school dominates family life, controlling the teen's waking hours through school, homework, and extracurricular activities. Think baseball or volleyball season.

This is not intended to be a statement of "good" or "bad." It is intended to look squarely at the situation in most of our schools. We are in charge. And even as we complain about the workload, we like it that way. At least, we make no genuine attempt to change it.

This means that we can also be highly realistic about the relationship we have with our school's parents. They are not fundamentally on "our" side; they are not a member of "our" adopted family qua school; they are not here to make us succeed; they are not paying tuition because it feels good. Our parents are here for one reason only – they believe it is good for their children. On that base of understanding, the school can have a fantastic relationship with the parents. Unfortunately, we find schools are constantly disappointed and even cynical about parents because they have unrealistic expectations of them. If we just accept them as selfish, interested primarily in their children, we will get along much better.

Selfish has a bad reputation. Proverbs 18:1 reads, "An unfriendly person pursues selfish ends and against all sound judgment starts quarrels." Philippians 2:3 reads, "in humility, value others above yourselves." That's not what we are talking about. We just recognize that the family is a special place like no other, and that the connection between the parents and the school is through the child. We also recognize that the family is under stress and that the school can be a strong support during the children's formative years. Often, indeed, the school is a stabilizing influence for its families, akin to what the church used to be. It is where many parents find their friends and where they find opportunities to socialize both in their children's activities and in meeting with each other outside the school.

Parents should be focused on their own children. No one else is going to be, at least not in that 24-hour, 365-days-a-year way! We shouldn't expect their attitude to be altruistic. We should understand their desire for the good of their children – insofar as we are able to deliver on our mission promise, the parent will support the school wholeheartedly, giving generously in time, advocacy, and money. We should also understand that when we do not deliver on that promise, the parent will stop supporting the school. This is most obviously evident after the child graduates.

With the child as the fulcrum of the parent / school relationship, we can have great confidence moving forward. For most children, most of the time, the school will do a great job and the parent will be happy, grateful, and generous. Occasionally, the school will not do so well and there will be a "divorce" with varying degrees of acrimony. It's not personal. It's because the parents are selfish about their child.

We advise therefore that our Christian schools continue to hope for the ideal represented by the statement at the beginning of this section. We advise the reality as well that religious, social, and economic trends place the school as the dominant partner in a child's upbringing during school age years, even as we acknowledge that the parent is still the key relationship for the child. The parent is relying on us. We advise that our relationship with the parent is based on the child-fulcrum and that we can expect a great relationship only and as we fulfill our mission promise.

Our relationship is year to year, even month to month. We can have great confidence in our parents to do what's best for their children, whether or not it's good for the school. Then we won't be disappointed at "lack of support" or "engagement." We advise that our attempts to engage the parent's support should be focused on and through the child whether it is in volunteering, giving, or serving. Then the "selfish" parent will be our best supporter.

Parents and Tuition: Investment or Sacrifice?

The words we use in our schools are very important. The Gospel of John begins with the words:

"In the beginning was the Word." The Word of God is called a "sword" (Revelation 1:16). The idea of communication is clearly an important Christian concept that is both abstract (language) as well as embodied (the person of Jesus). The story of the Tower of Babel is a reminder of the danger that language can pose. In our Christian schools, we must always be deeply sensitive to the words we use and the intended content / interpretation of those words.

Here, we apply this to the word "tuition." As CSM notes in other contexts, money and Christian schools have an uneasy co-existence. There is a sense in which our schools feel that money is a secular potential evil rather than a gift of God given for us to steward. Some are unabashedly apologetic about the need to charge tuition at all using language such as:

- We try to make our tuition as affordable as possible.
- We have the lowest tuition in our area.

Other of our schools are more neutral in tone, stating tuition and then providing clear reference to financial aid and other ways to defray the tuition cost. Few, if any, are "proud" of their tuition.

CSM suggests that tuition is a great good. The issue is not whether the tuition level is $6,000, $12,000, or $24,000. None of these numbers is "high" or "low." They are the "right" number if, as a result of charging it, the school can:

- provide resources that allow it to deliver the mission with excellence
- balance its budget
- compensate its employees honorably and respectfully
- provide a safe and optimal learning environment

- minimize / eliminate debt
- maintain a reserve

This is CSM's Ox Principle (see the Appendix).

Tuition, then, is a gift of God given to the school to steward in order to enable the Christian school to fulfill its God-given purpose – its mission. The relationship of the school to its parents is therefore neither one of apology (we are embarrassed we have to charge tuition), of supplication (we beg you to pay as much as you can afford), nor of fear (we hope our tuition won't turn you off our school). Rather, the school presents its tuition as:

- an opportunity for the parent to invest wisely in the lives of their children
- a responsibility to ensure the child is provided excellence, safety, and mission success
- a stewardship of the present to ensure the school's future

These ideas of opportunity, responsibility, and stewardship are powerful. We recommend that you clearly state this on your website. A statement on the tuition or admission page might read:

> CSM Christian School determines its tuition level annually to meet the needs of the school today and to ensure appropriate stewardship of the school's future through the Board's Strategic Plan. The Board and school's Leadership Team prayerfully consider the meaning of the school's mission and how that will come alive in the life of your child each year. Your tuition payment empowers our school to deliver an excellent program staffed by committed and expert faculty in a safe facility. We consider this to be a partnership with you where you are gifted the resources to invest in your children's future and we are held accountable for the

stewardship of the resources given to us through
the Board's Strategic Plan and the annual budget.

Similarly, we recommend that you include a statement in your
admission materials. Along with a descriptor of what the school
offers, great pictures of students in action, and validation quotes,
include a simple explanation of what tuition is and how it is spent.
A simple pie chart can illustrate how tuition pays for program,
people, facility, and strategic future developments reflecting
opportunity, responsibility, and stewardship. Along with the
printed / downloadable materials, include a video of the Head
of School / Principal in a short (less than three-minute) video
explaining the same thing.

In communicating verbally with current parents and prospective
parents, train the person who answers the phone, the immediate
contact on entry to the school, the admission staff, the teachers,
and the division leadership in the use of the language of opportunity, responsibility, and stewardship. Ensure that, if currently
present, the language of sacrifice is not in use anymore. A common
script might be put together so that the message is always the same
when the question of tuition arises. The following is an example
of a possible answer to the question: how much is tuition?

> Tuition is $6,800. It is an opportunity investment
> by you as parents in the life of your child. The
> school takes its responsibility seriously to steward
> your investment and provide excellence to your
> child. Tuition is set by the Board to ensure both
> present and future of the school so that your child
> will have an excellent education for all eight years
> your child will be at the school.

The re-orientation of language, and therefore thinking, from sacrifice to investment takes away the feeling of "loss" of money
the parent might experience rather than "gain" as a result of
investment. It gives everyone at the school great confidence in

the school's approach to stewardship. It focuses both parents and school / Board on the outcomes of tuition rather than on the money itself. The admission and mission orientation of the school therefore becomes much stronger. Tuition moves from barrier to opportunity.

This is equally true for families that cannot pay the full tuition. The same language applies to the provision of financial aid. The family invests what it can afford through a professional financial aid process and the school invests in the child to ensure access to a Christ-centered education. As CSM states elsewhere, the Christian school provides financial aid because:

- It derives from the Great Commandment.
- It helps the Christian school to operate without partiality, reflecting the nature of God.
- It reflects the commands of God to support the child, the parent, and the foreigner

Within the context of a strategic budgeting process, financial aid is also an investment for the school, not a "loss."

We encourage our Christian schools to speak about money with confidence. Of course, the "love of money is the root of many evils" (1 Timothy 6:10). Prayerfully considered as a gift of God for the school to steward, that same money becomes opportunity for the family, responsibility fulfillment for the school, and stewardship safeguarding excellence both in the present and the future.

Parents and Tuition: Affordable or Accessible?

Your school is not affordable. Get over it.

Let's look at some numbers. These numbers are taken from a variety of government and commercial sources using median 2019 numbers wherever possible.

We'll take a family with two children as our example. The parents earn $63,578 as household income before taxes. Both parents are working. This is roughly the median household income in the USA in 2019. What is left available for tuition once all the expenses are paid? The following table uses 2019 data and Iowa (a relatively low-cost state) as the state for comparison. The right-hand column provides the source for the information.

2019 Data				
Household Income	63,578			median household income USA
Expenses				
		Per	months	source
Mortgage ($200,000)	9,996	833	12	median 2019 - CoreLogic
Property taxes	1,858			Iowa median 1.29% rate
House insurance	734	61	12	spacesimply.com
Car payment (one car)	4,536	378	12	average - used vehicle - Motley Fool
Monthly car costs	3,936	328	12	average – AAA
Medical	6,859			MIT Living Wage Calculator
Food	6,358	530	12	thestreet.com
Federal taxes	273	23	12	us.icalculator.info (Iowa)
Iowa state taxes	392	33	12	us.icalculator.info (Iowa)
Social security	3,942	328	12	us.icalculator.info (Iowa)
Medicare	922	77	12	us.icalculator.info (Iowa)
Utilities	2,580	215	12	spacesimply.com
Internet	1,428	119	12	www.centurylinkquote.com
Other	6,378		12	MIT Living Wage Calculator
Charity	6,358			Tithing - 10%
Retirement	6,358			401K - 10%
Total	62,908			
Available for tuition	670			

It is clear that tuition is not "affordable" for this family. If they wish to send their children to a Christian school, and even pay full tuition for one of them, they will need to either scale back their tithing, retirement or make cuts in other spending. It is legitimate for this family to apply for and receive financial aid. This is a median family income, i.e, 50% of families make less than this family. In order to afford a $7,000 tuition, the family has to make $7,000 plus taxes ($8,500). This brings the income needed to $78,578. That is for one child. The arithmetic continues from there. It is not hard to see why families with six-figure incomes can legitimately apply for financial aid. For most families, our schools are not affordable.

If our schools are not affordable, can they be accessible, i.e., can we lower the bar for financial entrance such that most or all families can attend? The answer is, to an extent.

Our schools have two sources of revenues: tuition / fees and donations. CSM believes that the expenses of the school, for the vast majority of schools, should be paid for entirely through tuition / fees. Donations are intended to improve and move the school forward, not maintain it in place.

It is true that there are other sources of revenues such as rentals and other programs (before and after school, summer, etc.), but the amount of money they raise is small for the vast majority of schools. By and large, our schools do not have a third source of income. Some schools are supported by churches and some are run and owned by churches. The revenue provided by those churches and / or the costs that are not passed on, such as maintenance costs of the building, are just a special form of donation.

We acknowledge that the rapid growth of voucher programs in some American states and the provision of government funding in some Canadian provinces can be considered a third revenue stream (unless it is funded through corporate donations, for example, when it is another special form of donation). There are

154

troublesome aspects to such funding such as government oversight and political winds that have to be dealt with by the school from a mission standpoint.

So our schools are funded by tuition / fees and when families like the example above apply for financial aid, it means that they are not paying the full tuition. Very simply, if one family pays less, another family has to pay more. This is the source for financial aid. The equation is straightforward:

T+10% = T-FA

On average, the majority of families have to pay 10% more in order for other families to receive an average of 10% financial aid. The reality is that the actual tuition is higher by much more than 10% because the amount of financial aid actually given out is significantly higher than 10%, i.e., the individual financial aid for a child can range from 1% to 100%. Note that this financial aid includes multi-child discounts, which are financial aid by another name. In one school, fully 18% of the children were faculty children who received 100% financial aid (they paid no tuition), all of which had to be accounted for by the other parents in the school. Our data shows that a school can "afford" to give away 10% of its gross tuition (what the school would have received if everyone had paid the full amount) in financial aid.

While the school is not affordable, it can be made accessible therefore by raising the full tuition to allow for financial aid (discounts) that supports children whose families would otherwise not be able to afford a Christian education.

This is what such a budget looks like (from a CSM school):

Income	
Tuition and fees	2,243,593.00
Third revenue sources	73,265.00
Financial aid	(164,657.90)
Total	2,152,200.10
Expenses	
Wages and benefits	1,526,280.43
Operating costs	712,340.42
Total	2,238,620.84
Operations profit / loss	**(86,420.74)**
Donations	86,497.58
Total profit / loss	**76.84**

Strategically, the school will raise tuition so that the donations can actually be used to move the school program forward. Accessibility depends on tuition being at the level where it can support financial aid without crippling the ability to deliver mission delivery excellence and / or teacher compensation. The paradox is that the higher the tuition, the more accessible the school.

Nonetheless, where financial aid goes above 10%, tuition is unable to support financial aid. There are schools that attempt to do this but, in our experience, always by depressing compensation literally to a food-stamp level or by starving the program budgets. The further above 10% of gross tuition financial aid is set, the more donations are going to be crucial to support it. So for accessibility, the Christian school must also be sophisticated in its fundraising practices. This means two things:

1. Raising money by asking people for it, not by running events

2. Knowing and looking after the school's donors

Financial aid is a key part of the Christian school's outreach. Our schools are inclusive – they want to welcome all families to be part of the school's mission. Finances are a significant barrier to that. Financial aid has a strategic role to play in making your school accessible, even as it continues to remain unaffordable to most families.

Entry Grades: A Special Case for Financial Aid

Financial aid operates according to a budget and, when it is spent, then the school is unable to provide more assistance. This is one of those "rules" that is more often broken than not. However, in principle, it's a good discipline – and there are good exceptions to the rule.

One special case where CSM believes this should be waived applies to Middle and High School entry grades. It is imperative as a root of enrollment practice to fill entry grades.

The following chart shows an actual school's enrollment in the left-hand column. This school has done a great job to really fill its Preschool for the first time. However, many will not continue to Kindergarten because they are funded from a government program that is only for Preschool. However, the school will fill Kindergarten next year based on 16 coming from Preschool and demonstrated new demand. Next year then, the school will fill Kindergarten and that class will begin to wash through the school. In only six years, the school will be close to full. Middle School (sixth grade) is another entry point where the school always picks up five or so students, so even the smaller classes the school currently has will look a lot better in grades 6 – 8.

Grade	2019-20	Full	Missing	2020-21	2021-22	2022-23	2023-24	2024-25	2025-26
PK	42	42	0	42	42	42	42	42	42
Kindergarten	14	20	-6	20	20	20	20	20	20
1st	9	20	-11	14	20	20	20	20	20
2nd	15	20	-5	9	14	20	20	20	20
3rd	11	20	-9	15	9	14	20	20	20
4th	8	20	-12	11	15	9	14	20	20
5th	17	20	-3	8	11	15	9	14	20
LS Total	116	162	-46	119	131	140	145	156	162
6th	22	22	0	22	13	16	20	14	19
7th	17	22	-5	22	22	13	16	20	14
8th	13	22	-9	17	22	22	13	16	20
MS Total	52	66	-14	61	57	51	49	50	53
Total	168	228	-60	180	188	191	194	206	215

Full classes are obviously good from an academic point of view and a spiritual / social / emotional point of view. They provide a greater diversity of thinking, larger friend groups, more competition and potential for collaboration, greater pool of students for academic excellence. From a marketing perspective, full grades demonstrate demand. When grades are full, the school becomes more desirable and more families apply. It is a paradox that empty classes repel while full classes invite. The assumption is that a full school must be providing a superior education.

How should financial aid support that, even when the financial aid budget is spent? Consider the sixth-grade classes over the six years while the school is filling from the bottom:

	2019-20	2020-21	2021-22	2022-23	2023-24	2024-25	2025-26
6th	22	22	13	16	20	14	19
Spaces	0	0	9	6	2	8	3

There are five years where there are empty spaces. If financial aid could persuade an excellent mission appropriate family to enroll, then financial aid should be leveraged to whatever level is necessary. Here are the safeguards / cautions:

- The school only has to support the family for three years.
- It is unlikely that new students would come in grades 7 – 8.
- There is no additional cost, i.e., no new teacher is needed.

Even if the family came for "free," there would be a significant net benefit to the school from a full class – and a significant marketing benefit from being able to tell the community that families wanted to come to the school.

This reasoning would be true at ninth grade in a school with a high school. In a K – 12, it would partly be true at the Middle School entry grade as well. But not completely. The Finance Committee has to do important calculations to ensure that it is not putting the school in a long-term bind. Accepting the student means that you are committing to that student to the graduating year. Giving significant financial aid limits your ability to monetize that seat later on. The following example illustrates the potential dilemma:

Tuition is $8,500	Enrollment	Potential Enrollment	Financial Aid $	Students Receiving Aid	Average
K	20	20	28,000	7	4,000
1	18	20	3,800	1	3,800
2	17	20	38,700	9	4,300
3	17	20	21,000	4	5,250
4	16	20	34,300	7	4,900
5	16	20	17,850	5	3,570
6	18	22	12,360	3	4,120
7	17	22	44,800	8	5,600
8	17	22	14,920	4	3,730
9	21	24	8,400	3	2,800
10	24	24	40,800	8	5,100
11	22	24	32,100	6	5,350
12	22	24	31,120	8	3,890
Totals	245	282	328,150	73	56,410
Gross Tuition			2,082,500		
Financial Aid Percentage			15.8%		

It makes sense to use unbudgeted financial aid to fill ninth grade – there are only three empty seats, the students are only at the school for four years, it is unlikely that the school will recruit three students in grades 10 – 12, and there will be three more students for the athletics teams, the academic back and forth, to lead worship, and so on. There is no added cost to the school so there is no loss. Note too that it is important not to graduate classes with low financial aid and replace them with classes that have high financial aid. For example, the ninth-grade class in this example has little financial aid. If it is replaced with a class that has a more common financial aid profile, it will actually take almost four additional students to replace the revenue lost. Where you add financial aid therefore matters.

With this in mind, let's add six unbudgeted financial aid students to sixth grade and see what happens. In this example, we assume that the school typically adds an additional six students from outside the school at ninth grade. Filling the sixth-grade class limits the school's ability to add from the outside to just two. The arithmetic might look like this:

	6th	7th	8th	9th	10th	11th	12th	Income
If nothing is done	18	18	18	24	24	24	24	1,275,000
Add 4 FA 6th grade seats	22	22	22	24	24	24	24	
Additional income	0	0	0	2 students instead of 6				1,139,000

If nothing is done (no sixth-grade students are added using unbudgeted financial aid), the ninth grade will fill naturally and total income will be $1,275,000 across the six years. If, on the other hand, four additional sixth-grade students are recruited with financial aid (assuming 100% need), there will only be space for two full-pay students at ninth grade. Thus, while the school is now full from grades 6 – 12, there is a loss of revenue of $136,000.

Of course, the school may think it a small loss compared to having mission-appropriate students for seven rather than four years, and at a more impressionable age. And the school may see the loss as minimal when the market-competitive position is added to the mix. There is no wrong decision; you do have to understand what it means to add unbudgeted financial aid to the budget as a whole and be aware of the student's entire stay at the school, not just the year of entry.

This strategy works then when used at the school's final entry grade. There is very little risk, no additional expense, and the student body is enhanced. And it is very unlikely that these students will literally pay nothing – every dollar added is a bonus. However, at other entry grades such as sixth, fifth, Kindergarten, the risk is significant. The Finance Committee must have good spreadsheets to ensure that the school is not driving a significant income issue as these students move through the school.

Conclusion

Retention and recruitment are obviously linked in significant ways. The major difference lies in the reality of the relationships the current student already has in the school. All other areas overlap since they relate to communicating the school's excellence and ensuring that the school takes a child-centered and relationship orientation to its meeting with the parents and developing their mission-based relationship over time.

We hope that the redundancy in this book is helpful as you lead your school and can dip into various areas without having to go back and forth. We urge you to use this not just in the technical aspects of being a Family Relationship school, but in the training of staff and teachers in their roles in retention and recruitment.

We leave the final word to Scripture in Isaiah 29:

> Therefore this is what the Lord, who redeemed
> Abraham, says to the descendants of Jacob:
> "No longer will Jacob be ashamed;
> no longer will their faces grow pale.
> When they see among them their children,
> the work of my hands,
> they will keep my name holy;
> they will acknowledge the holiness of the Holy
> One of Jacob,
> and will stand in awe of the God of Israel.
> Those who are wayward in spirit will gain
> understanding;
> those who complain will accept instruction."

May your classrooms be full and your children joyful!

Governance – The Cord Principle

Ecclesiastes 4:12
"A cord of three strands is not quickly broken."

The Christian school includes 3 organizational partners who work
in service to the school's students:

1. The Board establishes the mission, hires the Head of
   School, holds the Head accountable for full classrooms,
   plans for the future through strategic planning and strategic financial management, and provides the resources
   (money and facilities) needed for that plan to succeed.
2. The Administration, led by the Head, fills the school
   responsibly, carries out the Board's plan, and supports the
   faculty to success.
3. The faculty serve the children, deliver the mission, witness to the action of God in the lives of children, and act
   collaboratively as a professional learning community. The
   staff support both Administration and faculty by engaging
   with resources and planning for their effective deployment.

In the same way, the Christian school includes 3 human partners
who cooperate in service to the child:

1. The parent(s) to whom God gives the responsibility of
   unity (the "two shall be one," reflecting the unity of God)
   within which the child grows safely, and through which

the child, known by God from before the womb, can fully develop God's intent for her or his life.

2. The teacher, who is the intersect (the relationship-in-action) of the school's mission with the child and who is fundamentally concerned with empowering the child's agency in interaction with the school's mission.

3. The Head, who stands as the guardian of the child's healthy development, the proactive partner with the parent, and the sustainer of the teacher's Godly genius.

These 2 sets of 3 strands (organizational and human) form the Cord Principle created by Christian School Management (CSM). Together, they are effective, and the school operates harmoniously. In conflict, or where the parts do not lift up each other's sphere, the school is in disarray and mission delivery is endangered. Let us discuss each of these in turn.

The Board of Trustees: This entity (sometimes also called the Board of Directors or Governing Board) has clear responsibilities and clear boundaries. *BoardSource* (Ten Basic Responsibilities of Nonprofit Boards, 2015)[13] writes that "strong Board leadership is fundamental to a strong and effective organization" (p. 11). This strong leadership is often construed as running the school. Nothing could be further from the truth or more destructive. We encounter far too many Christian schools where the Board continuously interferes with the operations side of the fence, directing school employees and negating the authority of the Head. This has also led the Board to arbitrarily dismiss the Head, even in the middle of a contract, and assume the Head's responsibilities at the Board level. The Cord Principle is emphatic that the Board's sphere is strategic: establishing the school's mission and using it "as the first frame of reference when making decisions" (p. 21); hiring the Head, who is the Board's ONLY employee, who must then be supported and evaluated (ch. 3); setting the school's "strategic direction" together with the Head and using that direction "for budgeting and other priorities" (p. 39).

There are, of course, other considerations for the Board – but if it can focus and do these 3 things brilliantly, the Board members can sleep easily at night. These tasks constitute the strategic function of the Board and can be contrasted with the operations function, which the Board is incompetent to carry out. This is an important understanding for individual Board members and the Board as a whole – as volunteers from many walks of life, the perspectives each brings to the collective table are invaluable. However, none is actually skilled in running a school and in running THIS school.

To avoid the "blind leading the blind" (Luke 6:39), the Board, for example, approves the budget, but the Head spends it; the Board identifies strategic priorities, but the Head executes them; the Board approves construction, but the construction company builds the building. The Board cord is both a strength and a potential noose – wise Board leadership understands the strategic / operations difference and leads strategically. This makes it a healthy organizational partner and allows it to contribute meaningfully to a strong and healthy school.

The second organizational partner is the Administration. It doesn't matter how small or large your school is and thus how many people are in the Administration. In some very small schools, it might be the Head, an admission / marketing part-time person, and a bookkeeper. In very large schools, the Administration might include the Head, a Chief Financial Officer, a Division Head or Principal of each division, a Family Relationship Manager (Admission Director), a Marketing Director, a Director of Development, an Athletics Director, and a Director of Guidance and College Counseling.

Wherever your school is, the Administration's task is as well defined as the Board's: deliver the mission with excellence, carry out the strategic plan together with its financial framework, be disciplined around the budget, maintain a safe school. And it is clear how this works – the Board determines the budget (and thus sets tuition) while the Administration spends the budget; the

Board creates the strategic plan and the budget to support it while the Administration implements; the Board creates and / or affirms the mission while the Administration interprets the mission in the light of everyday realities and uses it to guide and direct conversation and decision making. The Administration must be competent to run the school and, because no one was born with the skills to do such a complex thing, the Administration must also be committed to continuous improvement, thinking about administrative duties along spiritual, financial, organizational, curricular, and human resource lines and seeking to learn every day.

This is excellent modeling for the third organizational partner, the faculty and staff. Their primary task is to deliver the mission directly to the students / children of the school. This is sometimes lost on administrators who, being student-centered (cf. The Child Principle) think that they are also carrying out that task. Well, to some extent they are right. But they are not the Kindergarten teacher rolling on the floor all day with 5-year-olds or the music teacher working with choirs of 60 or 160 children in preparation for a worship service or a Christmas celebration. No, it is the teachers and the front-line staff (the assistants and the janitors and the lunch folks) who interact on a daily and minute-to-minute basis with the school's reason-for-existence, the children. Neither the Board nor the Administration can do those jobs, which are incredibly taxing and not always well compensated. We thus consider this partner the most *important* of the 3. The other 2 partners, Board and Administration, therefore have as their focus the support of the faculty and staff, and all they do is geared to that end.

The responsibility placed on the faculty and staff is glorious and also daunting: "The student is not above the teacher, but everyone who is fully trained will be like their teacher" (Luke 6:40). Their character and expertise must be beyond reproach. The science teacher, for example, must understand and really know science as well as be a Godly person. The 2 aspects of character and expertise must be constantly sought for and, as for all the partners, must be expanded through continuous professional renewal of body, soul, mind, and heart.

The 3 human partners form a cord within and around the 3 organizational partners and, of course, there is overlap. While these principles are primarily focused on the excellent operations of Christian schools, we must always remember that the students come to school, but they belong to their families. At the same time, this is a complicated relationship because the government has mandated that the child be educated, although that can happen in a variety of ways – home schooling, public and private schooling, to identify the basic methods. So the government mandates, the parent chooses, and the student goes to school. What is the importance then of the parent, and how does the parent fit into the cord?

There have been many learned books and articles written about this, and we make no effort to replicate or compete with them. We take a very practical stance. Parents are responsible for their children: "Children, obey your parents in the Lord for this is right" (Ephesians 6:1). And they are distinct from them: "Parents are not to be put to death for their children, nor children put to death for their parents; each will die for their own sin" (Deuteronomy 24:16). The school is responsible for the children through the contract that is signed and because it takes on legal responsibilities. For example, Garcia v. City of New York (1996) held that schools, once they take over physical custody and control of children, effectively take the place of their parents and guardians to both control and protect them. But schools have responsibilities beyond the parent because they act as representatives of the state. In this relationship, the Head takes a leadership role for her or his faculty and staff and has responsibility for mission delivery.

We would thus say that the parents' task is to choose a school that is consistent with their ambition for their child(ren). This is usually epitomized by the school's mission and values, and felt through the sense of community the Christian school has. Once that choice is made, the parent does not relinquish responsibility to support the school to effectively educate the child. At the same time, the parent must now submit to the school's authority, given to it both by the parent and the state: "Have confidence in your leaders and submit to their authority, because they keep watch over you as those who must give an account. Do this so that their work will be a joy, not a burden, for that would be of no benefit to you" (Hebrews 13:17).

That authority is localized in the Head, who has been appointed by the Board of Trustees and who has the power to both accept and reject a student. This authority is not unlimited, however, because at the end of each day the school gives the child back to the parent. This is why it is the Cord Principle – the 3 cords cannot be untangled without causing great harm to the child. The 3 cords must cooperate on the basis of mission and the Child Principle. When such cooperation exists, we typically experience the most powerful outcomes in the child's life.

The Christian School –
The Child Principle

Matthew 19:14
"Jesus said, 'Let the little children come to me, and do not hinder them, for the kingdom of heaven belongs to such as these.'"

Mark 10:14
"When Jesus saw this, he was indignant. He said to them, 'Let the little children come to me, and do not hinder them, for the kingdom of God belongs to such as these.'"

Luke 18:16
"But Jesus called the children to him and said, 'Let the little children come to me, and do not hinder them, for the kingdom of God belongs to such as these.'"

Matthew 18:3-5
"And he said: 'Truly I tell you, unless you change and become like little children, you will never enter the kingdom of heaven. Therefore, whoever takes the lowly position of this child is the greatest in the kingdom of heaven. And whoever welcomes one such child in my name welcomes me.'"

As the Christian school strives to implement the Child Principle, it recognizes that all 3 of the Synoptic gospels tell adults to stop getting in the child's way. The Child Principle, as defined by Christian School Management (CSM), requires the Christian school to:

- Put the child first (be student-centered).
- Instruct adults to meet the child where the child is first, before requiring the child to meet the adult where the adult is.
- Recognize that authority is there to serve the child, not to lord it over the child.

We need to be clear that child-centeredness is operating with the child at the center under the authority of God. Being child-centered should never be considered outside of the context of God's love and grace. First comes the recognition that we believe in God and that knowledge of God is primary: "Only be careful, and watch yourselves closely so that you do not forget the things your eyes have seen or let them fade from your heart as long as you live. Teach them to your children and to their children after them" (Deuteronomy 4:9). The cry to not forget is key to our status as a religion that is embedded in a teleological history centered in incarnation and resurrection.

But when we think of the child within the context of the Christian school, we quickly recognize that adults create school often to their own benefit, not to the primary benefit of the child. Let's think of a couple of actual examples:

- We create schedules that fit the convenience of teachers and administrators rather than the clear needs of the child.
- We teach in a way that is comfortable for me and reflects my particular style rather than fitting and meeting each child's unique needs and style.
- We allocate time to meet bureaucratic requirements and arbitrary rules (such as the 120-hour Carnegie Unit) rather than considering how much time – more or less – makes sense from the child's point of view.

We must remember that school is a mandatory place for children but an optional place for adults; it is a place where children have little or no power and adults have much. Children continually move through and have no necessary sense of permanence, while adults might stay for an entire career / vocation. It can be a place where well-meaning disciples "hinder" the children from coming to the Father.

Being child-centered makes us sensitive to our adult self-centeredness. Indeed, it is only within the context of God's love and grace that leaving the self-centeredness of adults behind makes any sense and, indeed, is possible. When we are able to stop being self-centered as adults, we are freed to become immersed in the lives of our children. Then, we can "teach (the laws) to your children, talking about them when you sit at home and when you walk along the road, when you lie down and when you get up" (Deuteronomy 11:19). This all-encompassing embrace of the teaching life is what turns it from mere career into vocation.

Of course, God takes the same approach, considering us His children, embracing us and being with us (Emmanuel) through the indwelling of the Holy Spirit, through the law written on our hearts, through the reality of knowing we are created beings, and teaching us (Psalms 25: 4-5; 27:11; 32:8; 86:11; 94:10; 119). He was with us at the beginning of time teaching the man (Genesis 2:16) while in Eden and apprenticing the man and woman in the making of clothing (Genesis 3:21). He came to us in Jesus, a child teaching in the Temple (Luke 2:46) and a man teaching the multitudes. In our schools we must note that God came to Adam and Eve within His creation and Jesus comes to us within the context of our lives. This is our model of how we should approach children – within the context of their own lives, teaching them where they are and in the way they can understand.

Child-centeredness thus asks us to leave behind our own adult selfishness (which scripturally is always attached to ambition, cf. 2 Corinthians 12:20; Galatians 5:20; Philippians 2:3; James 3:14). It asks us to come towards the child within the child's own context and in a way that makes sense to the child. And it asks us to exercise authority in order to serve the child, not to dominate the child.

We are reminded in our speaking of authority that Jesus remarked that we should receive the kingdom of God "like a child" (Mark 10:15) or not enter in. His last evening with his disciples was spent teaching them about foot washing. "Do you understand what I have done for you?" he asked them. "You call me 'Teacher' and 'Lord,' and rightly so, for that is what I am. Now that I, your Lord and Teacher, have washed your feet, you also should wash one another's feet" (John 13:12-14). Our authority is then to serve, a paradox in any age but no less in our own – where authority means to lord it over others and exercise privilege.

None of this is to take away the difference between an adult and a child, the person who has been trained and the one who has not, the administrator who has been promoted and the one who has not. All these reflect our talents and gifts (given to us) and their developmental growth. It is not to take away the authority that has the sense of judgment – there are plenty of places to go in Scripture to demonstrate the validity of that. But in our schools, the dominant impulse is always to look at education from the child's point of view, through the child's eyes, and with the child's best interests at heart. The dominant impulse is, thus, to love.

In our schools, that means actually paying deep attention to what we say we are doing and what we are actually doing; to recognizing our missions as being almost exclusively and correctly about helping the child; to asking children their thoughts, fears, dreams, aspirations and finding them of value and acting on them; to beginning each conversation with the admonition to keep the child at the center; to coming to decisions and asking the question as to whom the decision primarily benefits; to running meetings that focus on mission delivery to the child, whatever the topic of conversation.

Schools with children at the center are fun, happy, high achieving, extraordinary places. Adults in them are vocation driven, selfless, wise, pure. James warns against being a teacher, noting how many pitfalls there are. But for those who know that is their calling, he also encourages in James 3:13, "Who is wise and understanding among you? Let them show it by their good life, by deeds done in the humility that comes from wisdom. But if you harbor bitter envy and selfish ambition in your hearts, do not boast about it or deny the truth. But the wisdom that comes from heaven is first of all pure; then peace-loving, considerate, submissive, full of mercy and good fruit, impartial and sincere." That is the Child Principle.

Christian Management / Leadership: The Servant Leader Principle

"Jesus knew that the Father had put all things under his power, and that he had come from God and was returning to God; so he got up from the meal, took off his outer clothing, and wrapped a towel around his waist. … When he had finished washing their feet, he put on his clothes and returned to his place. 'Do you understand what I have done for you?' he asked them" (John 13:3-4, 12).

Christian school leaders are servant leaders. They have the following obligations:

- Serve the mission of the school – everything else is a subset of this.
- Serve the children of the school as the primary client.
- Recruit and support faculty and staff to:
    - provide resources,
    - be present for them and know each one,
    - be in an ongoing conversation with them,
    - help them grow throughout their careers,
    - hold them accountable, and
    - let them go when they are unable to fulfill their task with excellence.
- Partner with the Board for effective planning.
- Execute the plan with diligence and efficiency.

Authority and service seem to always be in tension. If I am in authority, how can I at the same time be in service? As the Head of School or Division Leader or Business Manager, where is authority and where is service? How do they link?

Authority is not to be denied. It is there for 3 important purposes: to know and do a job in such a way that people follow; to hold others accountable; to bring a key perspective to conversations and thus enrich decision making. Each of these purposes is part of leadership.

To be obvious, you can't be a leader unless you have followers. Gaining followers happens in a variety of ways, as history shows: the "strong" individual, the mystic, the rich person, the visionary, the person of power, and so on. Most of these are not servant leaders. It is important to know that – servant leadership is only one of many ways to lead. Christian School Management (CSM) considers it to be the highest form of leadership.

In a school, servant leadership operates at every level. The teacher needs to lead children from being subordinates to becoming followers as quickly as possible and does that through building relationships, demonstrating competence, teaching with passion, and having an expansive vision of where each child can go. The administrator optimally serves followers who are similarly committed to the mission of the school, are supported in their growing competence, trust in the leader, are held accountable, and contribute to the whole as members of a productive team. The Head serves the team by optimizing and expanding its strengths. Gallup, the polling organization, found that the 4 needs of followers were trust, compassion, stability, hope. In the Christian school, these words have resonance as well. Still, we might rewrite them in this form:

Gallup	Christian School
Trust	Competence and making and keeping promises
Compassion	Love – desiring always the best for the other
Stability	Knowing that Jesus is the Rock and standing securely there
Hope	Mission, planning, execution

Leadership does not always operate according to the organization chart. Formal leadership is often supported by informal leadership in the organization – the exemplary teacher who leads conversations, presents at conferences, and chairs committees has an authority far beyond her title. Informal leadership is the place where we discover those who have the servant's heart. While we may hire those who already have titles and / or reputations, we see in the everyday interactions of each person much more clearly what his or her impulse to action is – whether to power or to service.

Robert Greenleaf of the Greenleaf Center for Servant Leadership wrote: "The servant-leader is servant first ... It begins with the natural feeling that one wants to serve, to serve first. Then conscious choice brings one to aspire to lead. That person is sharply different from one who is leader first, perhaps because of the need to assuage an unusual power drive or to acquire material possessions ... The leader-first and the servant-first are 2 extreme types. Between them there are shadings and blends that are part of the infinite variety of human nature. The difference manifests itself in the care taken by the servant-first to make sure that other people's highest priority needs are being served. The best test, and one that is difficult to administer, is: Do those served grow as persons? Do they, while being served, become healthier, wiser, freer, more autonomous, more likely themselves to become servants? And, what is the effect on the least privileged in society? Will they benefit or at least not be further deprived?"[14]

This leads to the key observation that for the Christian school, servant leadership has an objective that is clear and non-negotiable. At the heart of the word "service" is the person of the child. We are not in our schools to serve everyone equally. Far from it. First is the child, who is the reason for the school, its mission outcome, and the most vulnerable person in the school community. Servant leadership is thus not even-handed. Within the context of the school, each servant leader serves first the student. Both the adult leader and the adult follower must know that their contract obligation to fulfill their responsibilities in return for various benefits is the legal mirror for their moral obligation to deliver the mission to the student.

The practical issues that arise are difficult in practice, while clear in theory. What happens if adults do not do their jobs well? How do we hold adults accountable for that mission delivery, irrespective of whether that is in the Business Office, in the classroom, on the playing fields, on field trips or in the Advancement Office? What about that beloved member of the church community who happens to be a mediocre teacher or administrator? Does servant leadership imply that we place adult community as the prime concern? Is rocking the boat being a servant? Should we overlook adult misconduct because we genuinely do care for every member of the school?

This would suggest that "servant" is a soft term with no substance. To the contrary – when we recognize that the center of our attention is the child, to serve the child implies that we are all accountable in the most demanding ways, both personally and collectively. In that collective sense, it is the school that takes on the responsibility for mission delivery to each child. Thus, the school must corporately take on the characteristic of servant leader to fully develop each child's God-given gifts and fulfill God's purpose in each child's life. Adults thus operate in 2 ways. The first is as an individual where the servant leader seeks to deliver the mission to the child and support, enhance, and develop the skills of each employee. The second is as a school body exhibiting corporately the servant leader disposition. Here, the requirement that each individual be a contributing element to that corporate identity is key.

If we are committed as servant leaders merely to the individual employee, it would be possible to imagine the needs of the adult becoming, as often happens in our schools, equivalent to or even greater than the needs of the child. Where, however, we are committed as servant leaders institutionally to the child, now each adult has a critical role to play and for which to be held account-able. Being a servant leader is thus not just an individual but a corporate responsibility. Note that 1 Corinthians 12 is implacable that we all play a part in the body of Christ and, implicitly, in whatever station of life we have been led to. "Even so the body is not made up of one part but of many" (v. 14).

The Head as servant leader primarily for the child must therefore root out adult incompetence and ensure that the child receives the best mission-centered education. Similarly, the Board of Trustees must hold the Head accountable. Once the highest needs of the child have been taken care of, and in order to achieve that goal, the adult is also nurtured and fed. Accountability is thus a key ele-ment of being a servant leader.

"Jesus called them together and said, 'You know that the rulers of the Gentiles lord it over them, and their high officials exercise authority over them. Not so with you. Instead, whoever wants to become great among you must be your servant, and whoever wants to be first must be your slave—just as the Son of Man did not come to be served, but to serve, and to give his life as a ransom for many'" (Matthew 20:25-28).

The Christian school is an exemplar of servant leadership. We give our lives as a school body to deliver the mission to the student. We are held accountable for the excellence of that delivery. I individ-ually deliver the mission and am held individually accountable. When the Christian school functions in this healthy way, it can achieve excellence.

The Christian School –
The Kingdom Principle

Matthew 6:10
"Our Father in heaven, hallowed be your name, your kingdom come, your will be done, on earth as it is in heaven."

Matthew 22:36-39
"Teacher, which is the greatest commandment in the Law? Jesus replied: 'Love the Lord your God with all your heart and with all your soul and with all your mind.' This is the first and greatest commandment. And the second is like it: 'Love your neighbor as yourself.' All the Law and the Prophets hang on these two commandments."

The Christian school is one that:

- intends for its children to bring God's kingdom "on earth as it is in heaven" (the Christian School Management motto)
- creates its mission carefully and delivers it with excellence, and
- recognizes Jesus as the Master Teacher.

In its simplest terms, the Kingdom Principle states that God gives us good work to do right here and now. This work is not menial nor does it merely fill in time until we go to be with the Father. Rather, God intends for us to do his will on earth, which has many rich possibilities and is individual to each one of us in our schools.

Many scholars believe that "on earth as it is in heaven" applies to each of the 3 preceding phrases, i.e., hallowed be your name, your kingdom come, your will be done.

In a Christian school, this principle is made concrete through the mission of the school. Certainly, theologically, from a church perspective, we could discuss the beautiful implications and applications of this prayer given to us by Jesus as the paradigm of prayers (including the injunction not to "babble like the pagans"!). But we are not theologians and our interest is in what this means in the life of a Christian school.

God's holiness, God's kingdom, God's will are made manifest in the Christian school through its mission. Don't be overwhelmed; within that context, the Christian school's role is to carry out its mission – and that is enough. The Christian school should not harbor ambitions that make the mission too bold. The mission should have authority, and it should be humble. The mission articulates clearly the purpose of the school and the purpose must be limited because we have limited money, people, facilities, land, students. We cannot do everything, and we are not called to do everything. We are called as a Christian school to do our mission.

Consider these slightly edited examples from real schools:

1. The mission of XXXX Day School is to assist the Christian family by providing an education marked by a biblical worldview and academic excellence so that students are equipped to be salt and light for God's glory.
2. XXXXXX Academy empowers students for leadership and service in our global society.
3. Within an atmosphere of love, concern, and mutual respect, XXXXXXX Preparatory School is committed to instilling Christian values, to developing future leaders, and to preparing students for college and lifetime learning through academically challenging programs and affirming competitive experiences.

4. XXXXXXXXX School develops in students a love of learning, respect for self and others, faith in God, and a sense of service to the world community.

5. The purpose of XXXX School is to enlighten the under-standing, shape the character, form the habits of discipline, and prepare young men and women to fulfill their God-given potential.

We note here that CSM does not judge the mission of a school. We recognize it as the human attempt of each school to bring God's kingdom into the lives of children here on earth, we respect it as such, and we hold the school accountable to do what it does to a standard of excellence.

We can see that these missions are very different from one another. Based on the school's founding history, its journey to this point, the challenges it sees and wishes to address, the children it wishes to serve, and its resources, the Christian school makes – and must make – a determination about its mission by both being bold and far-seeing in its vision and humble and limited in its reach.

It's hard to imagine the Christian school committing to a standard of mediocrity. But we have to understand that truly doing our mission at a standard of excellence comes with significant investment. Let's consider that by turning parts of the above mission state-ments into questions.

- How do we invest in "academic excellence"? Our children work hard in class and devote hours to further study. Our teachers provide engaging, faith-filled, relevant, practical, meaningful lessons – the work of a lifetime of application and study. Buildings that nurture the mind in a healthy environment conducive to imaginative and creative study can cost millions.

- What is the investment in "empowering students for lead-ership and service"? Leadership is not easily learned. It must be practiced in many situations, reflected upon, mentored by those who themselves understand and exemplify leadership. There can be significant risks that must be accepted in order for children to take on these tasks – loss of control, imperfect outcomes, mistakes. Service requires resources that could be devoted to "academic excellence"! If we are committed to service, those resources cannot be shifted to some other worthy objective.

- How do we invest in "an atmosphere of love, concern, and mutual respect"? At the least, it requires consistent and persistent modeling by people whose actions are authentic and grounded in a firm understanding of the love of Jesus. Students must be trained to put aside their natural self-centeredness and practice a different way.

- What is the investment that empowers children "to fulfill their God-given potential"? This might mean a willingness to explore and understand yourself and to discover what gifts God has given you. It means hiring teachers who delight and continually expand their own potential. It means the school's willingness for the child to fulfill a potential that was not in the school's plan, and maybe in a way that was not in the teacher's plan.

These are not simple things to talk about, let alone do. CSM has worked with schools that think of their mission statement as words rather than as God's call to bring His kingdom. We urge the Christian school to:

1. Prayerfully examine its mission and ensure that it truly represents the school's witness in the world.
2. Believe that the mission is sufficient, i.e., that the school cannot and is not responsible for everything.
3. Understand the mission in the light of the Kingdom Principle.
4. Ensure that the mission is embedded in the daily life and practice of the school.

When the Christian school takes its mission seriously, commits to its fulfillment at a level of excellence, and makes it meaningful daily, it will be in the best position possible to provide God's children with a glimpse of His kingdom.

Christian Teachers: The Love Principle

1 Corinthians 13:4-8a
"Love is patient, love is kind. It does not envy, it does not boast, it is not proud. It does not dishonor others, it is not self-seeking, it is not easily angered, it keeps no record of wrongs. Love does not delight in evil but rejoices with the truth. It always protects, always trusts, always hopes, always perseveres. Love never fails."

Zechariah 7:8-10
"And the word of the LORD came again to Zechariah: "This is what the LORD Almighty said: 'Administer true justice; show mercy and compassion to one another. Do not oppress the widow or the fatherless, the foreigner or the poor. Do not plot evil against each other.'""

Christian teachers provide an environment for their students that is loving and just:

- Just – not arbitrary or capricious – fair: allows the students to meet each interaction with an adult with certainty because the response to behavior or performance (good or bad) can be predicted irrespective of time or place; it is "Always."
- Loving – student-centered, not judgmental: goes to where the student is; assures the student that, whatever the circumstances, the adult has the student's best interests at

heart and will do whatever is needed for the student to be successful; it is Love incarnate.

It is good to remember the admonition of James that is, maybe, not spoken enough: "Not many of you should become teachers, my fellow believers, because you know that we who teach will be judged more strictly. We all stumble in many ways. Anyone who is never at fault in what they say is perfect, able to keep their whole body in check (ch. 3)."

That is not to say that James (and Paul in many other passages using δνιδάσκω) is talking about teaching in a Christian school! This is not a statement of theology. It is to say that we must seek hints as to the appropriate relationship between a child and teacher. James provides a significant insight that we can all associate with – the task of teaching is carried out with words and actions, and the way in which we use words and interact with children has enormous significance.

Today we think of that truism not just as the overt use of criticism or praise with the power to motivate or demotivate, but in elements of incredible subtlety. Consider the use of vocabulary that includes or excludes; the way words are supported – or contradicted – by body language; the exercise of authority versus power; communication preferences; communication methods, including technology; the giving and taking of responsibility; rewards and sanctions. Placing the student at the center of the conversation, i.e., focusing on the way in which students can benefit from our words and actions, leads to asking how completely a child can trust us. Here, we are not talking about truth and deceit (which are obviously important) but rather about the just and loving nature of our words and actions.

The Love Principle, at its heart, is about establishing a trust relationship. The writer of Titus says: "In your teaching show integrity, seriousness and soundness of speech that cannot be condemned, so that those who oppose you may be ashamed because they have nothing bad to say about us ... but to show that they [the teachers] can be fully trusted, so that in every way they will make the teaching about God our Savior attractive" (Titus 2:6-7).

It is important that we always recognize that the teacher in a Christian school not only wants the child to do well in an academic sense, thus securing a hopeful secular future, but also to be open to the Word of God and thus to have that secular future imbued with and infused with God's love, giving it meaning and eternal significance. We will not think of this as a biblical worldview (although that can be a useful phrase) but rather as the presence of God personally in the child's learning experience. The Love Principle brings the presence of God into the presence of the child. The teacher's trustworthiness is a model of God's trustworthiness.

God's trustworthiness can be thought of in this context as providing two feedback loops:

-   offering a true assessment of who we are – dead in our sins, and
-   providing the way through – making us alive.

As Paul says in Colossians 2:13: "When you were dead in your sins and in the uncircumcision of your flesh, God made you alive with Christ." We trust God because we know in ourselves that His assessment of us is accurate (we are dead in our sins) AND that He did whatever needed to be done (died and rose again) and told us how we needed to respond (your faith in the working of God – v. 12). It is this essential trustworthiness of God that the teacher echoes as a faint shadow in every interaction with a child. The teacher speaks truth in love (Ephesians 4:15) so that the child can mature. The teacher provides a true assessment and a solution at the same time.

Too many schools are far too individualistic in creating this environment of trust, one that consistently reinforces for students that ALL teachers are just / fair and loving / committed to students' success. The way individual teachers put these ideas into practice can vary so significantly that the environment is not empowering from the students' point of view. Instead, it may seem contradictory, even capricious.

The Love Principle, therefore, also supports the Christian Professional Learning Community. Through this approach, being just and being loving becomes systemic through the best practices of communities of teachers. In such a community:

- The student's development is the key measure of success, and the community's commitment to that is primary.
- Each faculty member's commitment to his or her own development is palpable.
- The willingness to engage in professional conversations as a norm of professional practice, unbounded by time or place, is endemic to the faculty culture.
- There is a common and unquestioned commitment to the mission of the school. There is generative conversation about the translation of that mission to every area of school life and to every developmental stage of the students.
- Study of the research and improvements in the practice of learning and teaching are valued. Best practice should imply a journey, not an ending!
- The faculty collaborate to ensure that their own improving practice is aligned (not identical) and that it is clear what is meant by curriculum, assessment, and standards.
- Faculty examine practice in their own classrooms and those of their colleagues, critique on the basis of student learning, and implement on the basis of continual improvement.

The Love Principle is both individual and corporate. It certainly is individual. Each faculty member is just (accurate and fair), while always supporting the student through thick and thin. As Jesus identified the failings of those around him, so he also drew people to himself so that they could be healed. While we are not so grandiose, nonetheless, we are an important echo of his ministry in the lives of our students. Through us, they will have a glimpse of the eternal. This principle is also corporate. We cannot do this on our own. Together with our colleagues (and assuredly with study and prayer), we must become a Christian Professional Learning Community where being just and loving is encoded in everyday practice, an environment in which learning becomes not just possible but profound for each student.

And that is the final point of this principle. It is not enough for us to do this for some, most, or even almost all students. As families are called to our mission and students enter our hallways, so our measure of success individually and corporately is 100%. Outside of circumstances where the student or family must be counseled out, our measure of success is absolute – all "100" students must be met, nurtured, and brought to a place of success. "What do you think? If a man owns a hundred sheep, and one of them wanders away, will he not leave the ninety-nine on the hills and go to look for the one that wandered off?" (Matthew 18:12).

The Love Principle looks easier than it actually is. To be just and loving every minute of every day of every week of every month of every year can only be accomplished through personal and corporate commitment to the task. "Finally, brothers and sisters, rejoice! Strive for full restoration, encourage one another, be of one mind, live in peace. And the God of love and peace will be with you" (2 Corinthians 13:11).

Christian Philanthropy:
The Mary Principle

Luke 8:3
"Mary (called Magdalene) from whom seven demons had come out; Joanna the wife of Chuza, the manager of Herod's household; Susanna; and many others. These women were helping to support them out of their own means."

Christian schools need supporters who will give of their abundance (at whatever level that indicates) in order to further the work of the school. While parents can be expected to pay tuition and fees for the services they receive, that money typically does not purchase property, build facilities, or provide items that are over and above normal everyday expenses. It is thus very important that Christian schools:

- raise money over and above operating income,
- treat donors honorably and respectfully, and
- follow the highest ethical standards.

From our perspective at Christian School Management (CSM), it is no casual statement to call this the Mary Principle. The women mentioned in Luke's Gospel had been "cured of evil spirits and diseases" (v. 2). They had experienced an astonishing change in their circumstances and were giving, we might assume, out of gratitude for deliverance. We can assume that these women were also the same ones who, in Luke 23 and 24, gave Jesus' body its final ministrations and were the first at the tomb the next day. Certainly, having someone as wealthy as Joanna in the ranks would have been enormously important in order to cover the expenses of this work.

Mary Magdalene is so important that she is mentioned at least 12 times, more than many of the apostles, and mentioned in connection with the key events of Jesus' life. These women were not just appurtenances, but key and vital members of Jesus' work with characteristics that one might find in other passages such as Proverbs 31. Connecting philanthropy to these women is to establish important points about the work of raising money for Christian schools. There are five operating principles that the Lukan narrative identifies:

1. Giving is in gratitude for what has been done.
2. Giving is done by people who are intimately involved with the action.
3. Giving includes involvement, not just the act of giving itself.
4. Giving galvanizes possibilities that otherwise could not be imagined.
5. Giving is recognized and honored.

We don't know if these women were asked to give or if they initiated the conversation. We can imagine, however, that once someone like Joanna had been healed, she asked in what way she could be part of what was going on with Jesus. There was obviously some kind of organizational structure to Jesus' ministry such that when he arrived at a place, there had been some preparations: food bought for the road, fresh clothing to replace what was wearing out, new sandals on occasion, even transportation such as the special time that Jesus told his disciples to seek out the ass for his entrance into Jerusalem. It can't have been a simple thing for 13 men and other followers to travel around the countryside living a peripatetic lifestyle. Joanna would have been gratefully welcomed into the company of donors who kept things on an even keel. Maybe she asked; maybe she was asked. What we do know is that she and others (many others) were thought important enough to be specifically honored through Luke's narrative.

Giving for Christian education needs to follow these five principles. Unfortunately, caring for the money of others has not been a strong practice on the part of Christian schools. Christian donors often (very often) become disillusioned because their money, given thoughtfully and hopefully, vanishes into a black hole that has these characteristics:

- It is not well accounted for or accountable – how was it spent and what was it used for.
- It does not solve problems; in fact, it merely papers over the problems the school fails to address. The consequence is that the need for the donation recurs.
- It does not move the school forward. It does not create space for creative solutions or visionary possibilities. Far from opening up opportunities, it reaffirms the school in thinking that its "faithful prayer" has been answered. The future is not a new day of creativity but only the present day repeated.
- It does not support building capacity in the administration, faculty, and staff of the school. The gift is used to cover deficits in the current budget. It does not fund "moving forward" items such as significant professional development, the use of consulting services, professionalization of operations, technology systems to collect and manage data.

Thus, Christian schools must manage and think about gifts in a different way. Even the manna in the desert enabled the Jewish people to move towards the Promised Land! Christian schools must know how to look after the gift legally and ethically. Christian schools must know how to use the gift in a way that moves the school from the present into the future. Gifts that only serve the present, by definition, mask underlying management and leadership problems that the Board of Trustees and School Head are not addressing effectively. Gifts are about the future and about vision and about direction.

Interestingly, Christian schools have trouble asking people for money. It would seem that Jesus and his disciples were not shy about it. Mary, Joanna, and many others supported their work. The Mary Principle suggests that many want to support the work of Jesus in the Christian school. Penelope Burk in her research into giving says that, for example, "9 to 10 percent of people say they have put bequests in their wills, but more than 30 percent say they would definitely do it or take under serious consideration if asked."[15]

It is clear that our schools do not have the confidence, or they do not think it is right, to ask their potential supporters for money. There is sometimes the thought that these people SHOULD give and we shouldn't have to ask them. We do not take a position on that. What we do know is that if the school does not ask them, many who would give will not. After all, they ARE being asked by many other organizations and individuals, sometimes on a weekly basis, to contribute to many worthy causes.

The Christian school needs philanthropic dollars. It is not a "love of money" that leads to asking for investment into the lives of children in the school. It is an appreciation of the need to serve the children of the school and carry out its mission. It is because the school can clearly and authentically identify a future-oriented need. It is done with complete integrity and open accountability. It is done transparently and without embarrassment. It is done with the operating budget taken care of – it is not a replacement for good daily management and accounting practices.

From the donor's perspective, the gift is given because it has been asked for. Donors feel that their philanthropy is an excellent investment in the future. They equally feel that they are honored in their giving – first, by being asked within the context of a plan; second, by being included appropriately in the conversation; third, by being thanked, told that their gift was used as asked, and given evidence that children benefited. Finally, the donor is treated in a way that makes him or her want to be equally or more generous the following year. A "tired" donor is typically someone for whom these things have not happened.

The Mary Principle is built on the Ox Principle. A school that balances its budget, limits its debt, compensates its employees professionally, and has a reserve is a school that is positioned to succeed in raising money optimally. The school that manages its budget poorly, fails to charge tuition that pays the bills, goes into debt, and asks its employees to work "sacrificially," i.e., without sufficient income to raise their families, is positioned to fail in any meaningful fund-raising. These two principles work hand in hand.

Every Christian family that is involved with a Christian school wants to support it. The Mary Principle, and the Ox Principle that underlies it, gives them every opportunity to do so. They will be eager and excited to see the miracles of what God has given them translate into the miracles that God will perform through their school.

Christian Finances – The Ox Principle

1 Timothy 6:17
"Do not muzzle an ox while it is treading out the grain."

Numbers 18:21
"I give to the Levites all the tithes in Israel as their inheritance in return for the work they do while serving at the tent of meeting."

1 Timothy 6:8
"Anyone who does not provide for their relatives, and especially for their own household, has denied the faith and is worse than an unbeliever."

Proverbs 22:7
"The rich rule over the poor, and the borrower is slave to the lender."

Exodus 41:33-36
"And now let Pharaoh look for a discerning and wise man and put him in charge of the land of Egypt. Let Pharaoh appoint commissioners over the land to take a fifth of the harvest of Egypt during the seven years of abundance. They should collect all the food of these good years that are coming and store up the grain under the authority of Pharaoh, to be kept in the cities for food. This food should be held in reserve for the country, to be used during the seven years of famine that will come upon Egypt, so that the country may not be ruined by the famine."

The Christian school thinks about money a lot. It enjoys the thought that God provides richly for His people. It wants to have the best resources it can to serve its children. It is neither embarrassed nor ashamed to talk about God's gift of money. The school has an obligation to:

- provide resources that allow it to deliver the mission with excellence,
- balance its budget,
- compensate its employees honorably and respectfully,
- provide a safe and optimal learning environment,
- minimize / eliminate debt, and
- maintain a reserve.

Let's start with the last item first: maintain a reserve. The Minnesota Council of Non-Profits discovered that "nonprofits with minimal or no reserves were more likely to have cut budgets, eliminated staff positions, reduced wages and benefits. They were also less likely to have been able to increase services to respond to growing demand."[16] That is, if your school has no cash reserves, it is in a constantly unstable situation, whether it needs to deal with economic hard times in a healthy way or to respond to economic good times by being able to take advantage of opportunities.

And there is no justification in the Christian school for taking the attitude that the Lord will provide. Certainly, there are times when the widow's jar of oil stays miraculously full. And we rejoice in the goodness of our God. At the same time, it is clear that trust can often (often!) be a misnomer for poor management, with the result that our schools go out of business because they lacked the cardinal virtue of prudence. Aristotle defined prudence as *recta ratio agibilium*, "right reason applied to practice." And St. Thomas Aquinas considered it the first of the virtues.

When we apply prudence with the guidance of the Holy Spirit, it may well lead us to take steps that may appear foolish from a worldly point of view – but that does not include the lack of foresight. Our God is a God of planning. Jeremiah 29:10 says, "For I know the plans I have for you," declares the Lord, "plans to prosper you and not to harm you, plans to give you hope and a future." Indeed, it is the ungodly who fail to plan: "Let us eat and drink … for tomorrow we die" (Isaiah 22:13).

Interestingly, that planning often meant that the great Christian leaders have often had to operate by faith that the plan would come to pass and not in their own lifetimes. So it is with our schools. Reserves are one of the ways in which the Christian school exercises prudence and foresight in order to ensure that the school will still be here for the next generation. Whether used or not in "my" time of service, they will provide Joseph's sustenance in the time of famine.

With that in mind, we can turn to the issue of the school's budget. Talking about money for the Christian school always begins with the school's mission. Many commentators have said that we should begin with the end in mind, and it is good advice. At Christian School Management (CSM), we would take it one step further and say that the "end" of the Christian school – its mission – is what dictates its budget.

Let there be no error here. Budget for many Christian schools means eking out a painful existence on the backs of poorly paid workers and badly maintained buildings. We don't have to go to the prosperity preachers to know that this is bad economics of body, mind, and spirit. There is no Christian character in being paid below the poverty level or not having the resources to teach with the right materials or passing the buck by deferring the upkeep of buildings and grounds.

The question thus becomes whether we believe in delivering the mission at a level of excellence and what that means. CSM believes that we are called to excellence, and that we witness that to our own people / community as well as to those who are watching us from the outside. "But you are a chosen race, a royal priesthood, a holy nation, a people for his own possession, that you may proclaim the excellencies of him who called you out of darkness into his marvelous light" (1 Peter 2:9). Witnessing to excellence means exemplifying excellence in our own financial practices.

There are then very clear steps to take in thinking about the budget:

1. Understand your own mission statement – what does it mean when we apply the standard of "excellence" to each of its words and think about the investment that is necessary to make that happen? (cf. the CSM Kingdom Principle)

2. Don't assume that the budget you have had for so many years is, de facto, the best budget. In fact, assume that there are deficits that you want to improve over time. As school leaders, be aware that our followers (employees) will want to act sacrificially in order to support the mission of the school and to help as many students as possible. Applaud that and appreciate it. However, don't let it stop the conversation about supporting them appropriately in their mission delivery.

3. Unless the school is new, debt is typically the wrong way to raise money.
   • This includes lines of credit required because there is not enough money to get through the year. Budgets must be balanced, and balanced by ensuring that the families who want this education cover the cost through their tuition.
   • When building improvements and new construction are needed, the money should be raised through fundraising.
   • Debt payments are a tax on tuition and degrade the school's budget.

4. The issue of compensation is important. It is just wrong not to compensate Christian workers professionally. The notion that they should be "underpaid" because it is a ministry fails to honor them. Certainly, it is a ministry. We will not try to define a fair wage. But we do know this: When our workers are paid at a level that does not allow them to raise a family, or that forces the them to rely on income from a spouse who works in a "secular" occupation, or that results in them not having benefits or any kind of retirement opportunities, then our budget lacks a moral foundation. We can go further and say that in order to attract and retain the best teachers and staff, we will pay them competitively, recognizing their value and honoring it.

A note about fundraising: CSM believes that the school's operational expenses must be paid for through tuition and fees. Fundraising is the gift of the heart that invests in the future of the school and to the direct benefit of the children. God has made us generous people. It is part of the way in which we are created. The school should joyfully ask its supporters for their gifts, given because of God's generosity to us (cf. the CSM Mary Principle).

We are committed to being great stewards of the riches that God gives to us. We need to think of God as generous and thus that He will meet our needs. We have a responsibility to express those needs in such a way that we exemplify excellence in our mission delivery, professionally pay and provide benefits to our people, maintain prudence in our reserves and debt management, and balance the budget. That is the Ox Principle.

The Church Year

In our daily lives we keep track of our activities and special events with a calendar. The church throughout the centuries has also "kept track" of days and seasons and commemorating special occasions with a calendar.

The Christian church has continued to follow the example set in the Old Testament of structuring the year around the marvelous acts of salvation that God completed for us in his Son, Christ. We call this structure the Church Year.

The Church Year calendar is organized into three sections: Sundays and seasons, feasts and festivals, and commemorations. The seasons of the Church Year are marked by specific liturgical colors to give us a visual reminder.

Found here are the Sundays and seasons in the cycles of the church's liturgical calendar: Christmas / Epiphany, Good Friday / Easter, and Pentecost, followed by the Season after Pentecost that includes Creation Time.

The Seasons of the Church Year

- Easter Season — 50 Days
- Easter Sunday
- Holy Saturday
- Good Friday
- Palm Sunday
- Pentecost
- Trinity
- Season of Lent
- September 1st Creation Time
- Creation Time
- 5 Sundays
- October 4th St. Francis of Assisi
- Ash Wednesday
- 4-8 Sundays
- Epiphany Season
- Season after Pentecost
- Epiphany
- 12 Days
- Feast of the Holy Innocents
- St. Stephen the Martyr
- Christmas Day
- 4 Sundays
- Christ the King Sunday
- Christmas Season
- Advent Season

CSM
partnership · leadership · transformation

The Marketing Page

OK, you're still reading. But remember, I warned you – this is a marketing page!

If you are a real leader, you never stop learning. Becoming a CSM member for a reasonable monthly or annual payment (christian-schoolmanagement.org) gives you access to advice that is different from all other advice. It is:

- specific to schools
- rooted in Scripture
- steeped in experience
- filled with practical, doable advice
- backed up by research in many fields
- tested in schools every year
- always updated when our faith understanding, the practical application, and / or research findings dictate

It also gives you access to CSM consultants for advice and counsel – fill in a form and, voila, responses provide you with options to consider.

Finally, membership makes you a partner to help schools like yours across the United States and Canada as we work **to reverse the decline in Christian education** and make a Christian education available to every child everywhere. Note: as long as maintain your membership, your monthly or annual payment never changes.

Consider how we might help you at your school through our consulting services, provided by Christian school leaders who are integrated into CSM thinking and CSM Principles. We never lose you money. If we were to boast, we would tell you that when we come to your school, you can expect an intellectual return on investment, a financial return on investment, and a spiritual return on investment. Talk to school leaders we have served and find out for yourself whether that's true. Our client schools are on our website.

We also currently have four publications. Think about buying them for yourself, your Board, and for your own school leaders for their professional growth. They include:

1. *A Call to Authentic Christian School Trusteeship: The Christian School Trustee Handbook* (2017)
2. *Stewards of Transformation: The Board President / Head of School Partnership in Christian Schools* (2018)
3. *The CSM Devotional for Christian School Leaders: A Journey of Challenge, Comfort, and Transformation* (2019)
4. Enrollment and the Christian School (2020)
5. The Stewardship of Sacred Time: Scheduling for Christian School Students (coming 2021)

Finally, consider whether you are carried to join with CSM in its mission. Call us if you feel God's tug on your heart.

The Three Metrics of a Christian Preschool

An excellent Preschool program can have a tremendous and unique impact on children for God's Kingdom. Here are two extracts from *The Philosophical Baby* by Alison Gopnik (a book that should be on every Preschool teacher's bookshelf – well-thumbed!). Both are from the concluding chapter "Babies and the Meaning of Life":

- "… for young children, truth-learning-epistemology and imagination-counterfactuals-aesthetics and love-caregiving-ethics are inextricably intertwined… babies love to learn. They learn by simply observing the unfolding statistics of the events around them… Children learn the psychology of those around them-their particular combination of beliefs, desires, and feeling, personality traits, motivations, and interests. They rapidly learn the rules that those around them follow, both the arbitrary conventions and the moral principles."

- "And babies can devote their attention and action to learning because they depend on the care of the people around them. Because we love babies, they can learn. Even more significantly, one of the central ways that babies and children learn is by watching what the people they love do and listening to what they say. This kind of learning allows children to take advantage of the discoveries of the previous generation. Caregivers implicitly and unconsciously teach babies at the same time as they care for them."[17]

The first reason to have Preschool is therefore straightforward: this is a highly formative time of life and is an incredibly important opportunity to influence the child in dramatic formative ways. However, if Preschool is literally preparing the baby / child for school, then it would be better not to have it. Let's listen to Dr. Gopnik again from an interview she gave:

> "The preschool years, from an evolutionary point of view, are an extended period of immaturity in the human lifespan. But it is during this period of immaturity that exploration and play take place. Ultimately, exploration and play during preschool turns us into adults who are flexible and sophisticated thinkers. If you look across the animal kingdom, you'll find that the more flexible the adult is, the longer that animal has had a chance to be immature. I think that even the term preschooler is a bit misleading. It implies that our job is to get children ready for school and that school is where the important things happen. But preschool isn't just about readiness. It's an important entity in its own right. Indeed, what preschool teachers do is arguably more important than what occurs in the elementary school. And I think we have lots and lots of evidence of that now."

For Preschool to have appropriate and developmentally strong impact, the Christian school must resist the move of society to push "academics" downward, to eliminate natural play, to layer learning requirements on the baby / child as if it were a machine. One website puts it (appallingly) in this way:

> "Yep, your child will be prepping for Kindergarten in preschool. This means your preschooler will

start to learn the foundations of math! That generally includes numbers from one to ten, counting up
to ten or even twenty, and even that numbers and
objects correspond."

The problem we always face in our schools is that children are
highly adaptable mammals who will do what the older person
tells them to do. The effective Preschool is very much a child-centered, not adult-centered environment. Far from a "structured
learning environment" (code for adults in charge), the Christian
Preschool must be child-centered with a focus on exploration and
play. Maria Montessori observed the same thing. Her Nido / Infant
Community / Casa provided an environment that gave the child
agency, uninterrupted work flow, support from the teacher-guide
rather than direction, no grades, no rewards, no punishment, and
a large peer group (c. 30) composed of at least three years of age.

The Christian Preschool thus has two educational reasons for being:

- its formative capacity
- its willingness to be counter-cultural in meeting the child
  where the child is

Does the Christian Preschool have a business rationale?

While the school mission is the same for Preschool as for the K
– 12 program, the Preschool / childcare industry is unique in several ways. First, Preschool is price sensitive in a way that K – 12
tuition is not. The Preschool market tends to be highly competitive, follow similar models in pricing and programs, and enrollment depends highly on location. A nurturing, safe, environment
tends to be at the top of the list for parent needs during this stage
of child development. Because parents think largely of Preschool
as "daycare," they tend to think of it as dealing with a problem
rather than providing an opportunity. They want to pay as little as
possible and are not deeply thoughtful about the benefits / challenges of any individual program. There are, of course, parents

who want their child to progress and get a head start on the competition in the game of life – still at a low price! So Preschool can be a difficult program to manage financially and is an enterprise in which you can easily grow yourself out of business. Hourly staffing and maintaining ratios can provide a unique challenge compared to the usually fixed schedules of K – 12 faculty and staff. Managing those hours and ratios is the most important component of financial sustainability. Most Preschools, properly accounted, lose money. It is hard to run a Preschool really well, paying skilled teachers market value, at a price parents are willing to pay. The younger the child, the lower the child / adult ratios and the bigger the financial loss!! From a business point of view, it is not typically worth running a Preschool program.

While the immediate business model is somewhat lacking, if thought of longer term, the business model makes more sense. This is where the Christian Preschool feeds into the K – 12 program. For this to happen, the teachers must:

- execute the mission of the school
- understand the connections between the Preschool program and the K – 12 faculty and staff regarding mission language and its application to all decision making

Administrators must price it correctly – not to ensure the highest number enrolled (every student might be losing you more money) but to ensure the highest possible number moving through to the Kindergarten class. This typically means raising the price until those who are looking at the school from a daycare point of view, not from a mission point of view, have left.

Pricing a Preschool program should lead to a profit margin that contributes to the overall operational excellence of the school. Executing a successful Preschool program requires administrative support in the areas of marketing, accounts payable and receivable, and human resources. Preschool income should cover direct expenses, and then contribute to these general schoolwide administrative expenses as well. A simple example from a school follows:

Preschool	1:12 ratio
Children	12
Cost	7,900
Income	94,800
Teacher	50,000
Aide	25,000
Cost	75,000
Profit	20.9%

The three metrics therefore are:

1. A formative and child-centered program
2. At least a 60% re-enrollment rate
3. A 20% profit margin on actual direct running costs

Having a Christian Preschool program is a powerful witness in the community and an important influence in the life of the child. Well-constructed programs that meet the three metrics are a valuable part of any Christian school.

References

1   United Nations. (1989). *United Nations Convention on the Rights of the Child*. https://www.ohchr.org/en/professionalinterest/pages/crc.aspx.

2   Putnam, R. (2015). *Our Kids: The American Dream in Crisis*. Simon and Schuster.

3   Verdery, A. M., & Margolis, R. (2017). Projected Kinlessness in the United States. *Proceedings of the National Academy of Sciences, 114*(42), 11109-11114. doi: 10.1073/pnas.1710341114

4   McLanahan, S. (2011). Family Instability and Complexity After a Nonmarital Birth: Outcomes for Children in Fragile Families. In M.J. Carlson and P. England (Eds.), *Social Class and Changing Families in an Unequal America* (pp. 108-133). Stanford University Press.

5   Barna Group. (2019). *Households of Faith: The Rituals and Relationships That Turn a Home Into a Sacred Space*. Barna Group.

6   Harris, A. L., & Robinson, K. (2016). A New Framework for Understanding Parental Involvement: Setting the Stage for Academic Success. *The Russel Sage Foundation Journal of the Social Sciences, 2*(5), 186-201. https://muse.jhu.edu/article/633742/pdf

7   US Department of Education. *Diversity & Opportunity*. Retrieved August 6, 2020, from https://www.ed.gov/diversity-opportunity

8   Wile, A. J., & Shouppe, G. A. (2011). Does Time-of-Day of Instruction Impact Class Achievement?. *Perspectives in Learning: A Journal of the College of Education & Health Professions, 12*(1), 21-25. http://csuepress.columbusstate.edu/pil/vol12/iss1/9

9   Kelley, P., & Lee, C. J. (2014). *Later School Start Times in Adolescence: Time for Change.* Education Commission of the States. https://digitalcommons.law.umaryland.edu/home_sec_fac_pubs/1/

10 Sievertsen, H. H., Gino, F., & Piovesan, M. (2016). Cognitive fatigue influences students' performance on standardized tests. *Proceedings of the National Academy of Sciences, 113*(10), 2621-2624. doi: 10.1073/pnas.1516947113

11 Kane, T. J., McCraffrey, D. F., Miller, T., & Staiger, D. O. (2012). *Have We Identified Effective Teachers?: Validating Measure of Effective Teaching Using Random Assignment.* The MET Project.

12 ChildStats.gov. (2018). *POP1 Child Population.* https://www.childstats.gov/americaschildren/tables/pop1.asp

13 Ingram, R. T. (2015). *Ten Basic Responsibilities of Nonprofit Boards.* BoardSource.

14 Greenleaf, R. K. (1970). *The Servant as Leader.* The Greenleaf Centre for Servant Leadership.

15 Burk, P. (2018). *Donor-Centered Fundraising.* Cygnus Applied Research, Inc.

16 Aanestad, K., Pratt, J., & Bemis, C. (2018). *Nonprofit Current Conditions Report.* Minnesota Council of Nonprofits.

17 Gopnik, A. (2010). *The Philosophical Baby: What Children's Minds Tell Us About Truth, Love, and the Meaning of Life.* Picador.

CPSIA information can be obtained
at www.ICGtesting.com
Printed in the USA
JSHW031325141120
9580JS00001B/1

9 781632 213761